DATE DUE

The American West

People, Places, and Ideas

The American West

People, Places, and Ideas

BY SUZAN CAMPBELL

WITH AN ESSAY BY KATHLEEN E. ASH-MILBY

ROCKWELL MUSEUM OF WESTERN ART

WESTERN EDGE PRESS

Copyright © 2001, Rockwell Museum of Western Art, Corning, New York

Distributed by Western Edge Press, 126 Candelario St., Santa, Fe, NM 87501
      westernedge@santa-fe.net • phone/fax: 505.988-7214

ISBN: 1-889921-13-0 paperbound   •   ISBN: 1-889921-14-9 hardbound

Library of Congress Catalog Card Number: 01-130235

Poem on page 126 reprinted from *First Indian on the Moon*, © 1993 by Sherman Alexie, by permission of Hanging Loose Press

Design and production by Jim Mafchir, Western Edge Press

Printed in Hong Kong

Rockwell
Museum of
Western Art

The Best of the West
in the East!

Photography credits

Frontispiece:
    Plate 1. Truman Lowe, *Feather Basket*, 1989. Bronze (2/12), 14 x 18 x 9 inches. Gift of Marcia D. Weber and James B. Flaws. 2000.21

FRANK BORKOWSKI: PLATES 1, 3, 5, 6, 9, 15, 19, 20, 25, 26, 30, 32, 33, 34, 36, 37, 38, 39, 40 41, 42, 44, 46, 47, 48, 50, 52, 53, 54, 58, 59, 62, 63, 64, 65, 75, 76, 77, 79, 80, 81, 84, 87, 88, 89, 90, 91, 94

JAMES O. MILMOE: PLATES 2, 7, 8, 10, 11, 12, 13, 14, 16, 17, 21, 23, 24, 27, 28, 29, 31, 43, 45, 49, 51, 61, 67, 68, 69, 72, 74, 78

CHARLES SWAIN: PLATES 4, 35, 66, 70, 71, 82, 86

NICK WILLIAMS: PLATES 18, 22

ERIC SWANSON: 56

EMIL GHINGER: 57

Table of Contents

2. Walter Ufer, *Along the Rio Grande*, 1920. Oil on canvas, 24½ x 24½ inches. Gift of Robert F. Rockwell, Jr. 78.70

I paint the Indian as he is. In the garden digging—In the field working—Riding amongst the sage—Meeting his woman in the desert—Angling for trout—In meditation.

—Walter Ufer, 1928, in Laura M. Bickerstaff, *Pioneer Artists of Taos*

Acknowledgments

The West *is* America. Its artists—the earliest Native American artists who left behind their petroglyphs, the explorer artists of the nineteenth century who fired the imagination of Easterners with their romantic visions, the artists of various ethnic cultures who have chosen the West as their home, the contemporary artists who interpret our culture, and so many others—tell our story. The distinctive qualities of our Americanness are reflected in their art more than in any other.

How incredibly fortunate we are to have a splendid collection of western and Native American art here in Corning, New York—an area that was once a part of the American frontier but has been solidly a part of the East for about two centuries. Truly, we have "the best of the West in the East." We have a wonderful opportunity to exploit this art in the cause of learning and delight, and, as I see it, an obligation to use our collection as a spur to stimulate discovery, introspection, discussion, and the healthiest kind of debate. And that's exactly what the Rockwell Museum's Board of Trustees set out to do when we began to reinvent this Museum. We sought to create a place that was warm and inviting and that felt like the West—a comfortable place where people would come again and again, lured by its art and ambiance. In short, we wanted our treasure—our art—to yield all possible dividends.

In our plan to become the new Rockwell Museum of Western Art, our focus was solely on western and Native American art, expressed through an interpretive plan which made the art come alive for visitors. We acquired art that broadened the scope of our existing collection. New educational programs were created to spark the imagination. Finally, in our beautiful, historic building, we designed an entirely new environment that provides an inviting destination for visitors and an outstanding setting for our art.

Now that we have put the finishing touches on several years' hard work of reinventing the Rockwell Museum as the Rockwell Museum of Western Art, we are delighted to present the results of our efforts as we celebrate our 25th anniversary in 2001. With this catalog, we share highlights of our collection and offer a sense of what this "new" museum is all about.

The task of reinventing a museum is no small one. Creating an imaginative vision and transforming it into reality requires the time, talents, and dedication of many people. My deepest thanks to the many individuals who contributed time, thought, creativity, and support to the project.

In particular, I'd like to thank the museum's Interpretive Team. Guest Curator Suzan Campbell, who authored the text for this volume, ably led us through the creative process with enthusiasm and unwavering focus on the outcome. Curator and catalog essayist Kathleen E. Ash-Milby constantly expanded our views of Native American art and challenged the museum to question traditional assumptions. Historian Christopher Clarke held us to high standards of historical accuracy throughout.

My deepest gratitude, too, to the museum's original visionaries. Bob and Hertha Rockwell generously chose to share their passion for western art and many outstanding works from their personal collection with others. Their original gift remains the core of our present collection. Over the years, Bob and Hertha and their children, Sandra Rockwell

Herron and Robert (Bobby) Rockwell III, have remained tireless supporters through their ongoing contributions of art, time, and leadership. Without them, this museum simply would not exist.

Nor would it exist without major financial support from the company once known as Corning Glass Works, now Corning Incorporated. A quarter of a century ago, CEO Amory Houghton shared Bob Rockwell's vision and committed the resources to make it a reality. Since then, Corning has been a steadfast patron of the museum and its programs, including contributions of in-kind services and talent. We have benefited enormously from the skills and talents of Corning employees who were deeply involved in our reinvention: Bob Condella, Jim Laudenslager, Ralph Ely, Bob Hairston, and Al Venette, as well as the many other Corning employees who have supported us over the years.

I am also personally indebted to the Museum's Board of Trustees for their bold support of our new direction. I especially want to thank Board President Kristin Swain for her unwavering dedication to the museum. Kristin's guidance, patience, wisdom, and friendship have been invaluable. The Steering Committee, serving under Kristin's able leadership, was instrumental in ensuring the success of this project, and I'd like to express my gratitude to each of its members: Jim Flaws, Bryan Lanahan, Marie McKee, John Peck, Ann Weiland, and David Whitehouse.

I'd also like to say a special thanks to Rick Stewart, Director of the Amon Carter Museum in Fort Worth, Texas, and President of Museums West, and to members of that consortium: the Autry Museum of Western Heritage, Buffalo Bill Historical Center, Eiteljorg Museum of Amer-

Kenneth Miller Adams, *Woman and Boy Drinking*, date unknown, lithograph on paper (99.28.1) Clara S. Peck Fund purchase.

ican Indians and Western Art, Gilcrease Museum, Glenbow Museum, The Heard Museum, National Cowboy and Western Heritage Museum, and The National Wildlife Art Museum. Leaders at each of these museums encouraged us throughout our project. Likewise, noted scholar Peter Hassrick gave us the benefit of his vast knowledge of western art throughout the project. And our own Trustee, the noted painter and former museum director Tom Buechner, not only provided this volume's preface, but contributed in many ways to our vision for the future.

The contributions of architects and designers Jim Czajka, John Boyer, and Ryan Koslowski of Allanbrook Benic Czajka Architects and Planners, New York City, are less visible in this volume, but the results of their talents are apparent throughout the Museum. I greatly appreciate their leadership, creativity, and sensitivity. Jim, John, Ryan, and their team of experts united our past and future in the extraordinary setting they developed for the museum's art. Likewise, our general contractors, Welliver McGuire Inc., led by Mike Martin, John DeGraw, and Mike Schamel, were diligent partners in the process, ensuring that the construction adhered to design specifications, and that materials and workmanship were of the highest quality. All of these individuals honored not only our vision and treasured collection but also the original character of the building that is our home—once Corning's City Hall, and a generous gift from the City in 1981.

I'm also grateful to Scott Hanson and his colleagues at The Rudder Group in Toronto for their gentle yet persistent guidance, valuable insights, and business acumen. Scott and his team steered us on a steady, reasoned course with the utmost calm and tact throughout.

As important to the Museum as these valued experts are our many members, contributors, docents, and volunteers who demonstrated their belief in this Museum for many years and have enthusiastically embraced its new direction. These people are our core and a major reason for our existence.

Finally, I want to say a special and very warm thanks to our wonderful staff: Sue Bodemer, Melissa Carlson, Butch Hoffmann, Dan Hoffmann, Joyce Penn, Robert F. Rockwell III, Jean Shumway, Tom Tunnicliff, Kacie Tuma, Cindy Weakland, and Judy Wright. Their dedication to our vision was surpassed only by their patience with an environment of perpetual change as we worked to achieve it. Their daily efforts are the hidden but truly essential strength of the Museum.

Ultimately, all of us who worked on this project came together around a single purpose and vision. We were all deeply aware that it is the artists who have created such wonderful and compelling works. Thus, we all share a sense of extraordinary gratitude to these diverse and gifted individuals. Here at the Rockwell Museum of Western Art, we are delighted and honored to share their vision with a public eager to embrace it. Do come, and let us give you a warm, western welcome!

—Stuart A. Chase
Director

3. Frank Earle Schoonover, *Ojibway Indian Spearing the Maskenozha (Pike)*, 1923. Oil on canvas, 40⅛ x 30⅛ inches. Clara S. Peck Fund purchase. 97.1

Preface

Bob Rockwell and I met in 1951 at a Rotary Club lunch here in Corning. I knew that he was from Colorado and that he and his wife, Hertha, ran Rockwell's Department Store on Market Street. Twenty years later, that store was brimming over with paintings, bronzes, guns, buffalo skulls, Indian blankets, old toys, and a huge collection of Steuben Glass (made by or under the auspices of Bob's old friend Fred Carder). It was an extraordinary place to buy a sweater.

In 1976, the Rockwell Museum was established by Corning Glass Works, and most of the wonderful things that used to be between the racks and above the counters of Rockwell's Department Store were installed in the new galleries. At the grand opening, what the Rockwells had quietly accomplished suddenly became evident: They had brought the best of the West to the East, to Corning, New York. In little more than a decade, they had built a major collection of Remingtons and Russells, of Bierstadts and Farnys, of Thomas Morans and W. R. Leighs. They had spanned the field from Seth Eastman's 1848 painting, *The Tanner* (Plate 49), to *The Buffalo Hunt*, by Bob's friend Nick Eggenhofer, who painted it in 1960.

The following pages of this catalog describe the richness and quality of this collection but not its breadth. Bob Rockwell's love of the West is

Fig. 1 Bob Rockwell, Jr. on his pony at the Rockwell's Double "H" Ranch in Colorado, 1915. Rockwell Family Collection.

intense, personal, and focused. His collection is inspired by his own vision of the subject and includes a vast array of paintings, drawings, prints, letters, and artifacts that document the West as he sees it. His acquisitions comprise an impressive self-portrait. Not only do they collectively describe his passion, tastes, and interests but also his knowledge, thoroughness, and capacity to learn. He looked, read, and compared; he sought and found the best advice available from experts in both museums and in the marketplace. He took risks but he bought well, and today we are the beneficiaries.

I traveled with Bob in the West on several occasions. When we stopped to see a collection or visit a museum we were always among friends. He was known and liked everywhere; a good listener and a better storyteller, he charmed us all with his plain-spoken enthusiasm. Miss Peck is a prime example.

Clara S. Peck was a New Yorker with a passion for the West. She was elderly when she met Bob early in the 1970s and had given up horse breeding and her annual trip to an Indian reservation where she had a residence. Her New York apartment contained impressive paintings by George Catlin and Alfred Jacob Miller, and a remarkable set of books including *The Oregon Trail*, illustrated by Charles M. Russell. Bob and she became good friends, and in 1983 she gave the Rockwell Museum $3 million with which to establish the Clara S. Peck Fund. (At her death in 1983 the Museum received her western books and pictures.) Over the years, interest from the Peck Fund has been used to buy works of art for the Museum. Outstanding among these is Ernest Blumenschein's *Jury for Trial of a Sheepherder for Murder* (Plate 73), (1936), which it acquired in 1997.

The Museum's extraordinary collection of western art grows and blossoms in Corning, New York, because it is supported by Corning Incorporated, formerly Corning Glass Works. Recently transformed into the Rockwell Museum of Western Art, the entire building is now devoted to this single subject, not as a defined moment in history or as a geographic area but as an evolving concept which influences, inspires, and entertains all of us.

—*Thomas C. Buechner,* Former Director, Rockwell Museum; Member, Board of Trustees, Rockwell Museum of Western Art

Fig. 2   Bob and Hertha Rockwell. Rockwell Family Collection.

4. Charles Marion Russell, *Stolen Horses*, 1898. Oil on academy board, 18 x 24 inches. Gift of the Rockwell Foundation. 78.57

IN THE OLD DAYS men did not read much but were all good story tellers and many of their lives would have made a romance. Although Mr. Russell is a good story teller he is also a good listener and has a remarkable memory for detail. The stories he heard were history that has never been written and would have been lost had he lacked the ability to put them on canvas. . . . Mr. Russell lives in the past as you all know, and when civilization crowds too close . . . he takes his coat and hat, his tooth brush in his pocket and goes to Mr. Matheson's ranch near Belt, where the Highwood mountains loom up big and the Belt range make wonderful pictures in the evening sun. At this ranch the artist is a boy. . . .When the dishes are washed he will, in nice weather, climb a hay stack and from that elevated place imagine that stretch of country back before the white man came, with Indians and their land alive with game. He goes into what his red brothers would call "The Great Silence" where nature teaches her child. When he comes back from one of these visits I have seen him start three big pictures within one week.

—Nancy (Mrs. Charles) Russell, 1914, in Peter H. Hassrick, *Charles M. Russell*

THE COLLECTION

5. Alfred Jacob Miller, *Crow Indian on Horseback*, 1844. Oil on canvas, 19 1/4 x 25 3/8 inches.
Clara S. Peck bequest. 83.46.17

The friendly and flowing savage, who is he?
Is he waiting for civilization, or past it and mastering it?

—Walt Whitman, *Song of Myself 39*, 1855, 1881

I use western
methods in the
process of creating a
personal language
needed to explore
the traditions of my
culture. References
to serpents,
animals, flowers,
and branches reveal
but do not totally
expose the mysteries
or meanings of
Yaqui culture.

—Mario Martinez
Indian Artist,
Fall 1998

6. Mario Martinez, *Yo Chiva`ato (Enchanted Goat),* 1995. Oil on canvas, 56 x 54 inches. Clara S. Peck Fund purchase. 2000.37

BY SUZAN CAMPBELL

The American West
People, Places, and Ideas

The true point of view in the history of this nation is not the Atlantic coast, it is the great West.

—Frederick Jackson Turner, in *The Significance of the Frontier in American History*, 1893[1]

THE WEST! THE GREAT AMERICAN WEST! These powerful words conjure up visions of a familiar yet remotely exotic region that symbolizes essential American spirit and character. But where, exactly, *is* the American West? And *what* is it? Is there *an* American West, or are there *many* Wests?

Today, hundreds of years after settlers landed on the eastern shores of America and fixed their gazes toward the western horizon that promised a New World Eden, we realize that the West is more firmly located in our hearts and imaginations than in a particular geographic region. When considered through time as well as space, the West embraces the entire North American continent and its history. Indeed, America *is* the West.

When historian Frederick Jackson Turner presented his influential "frontier thesis" to members of the American Historical Association in Chicago more than one hundred years ago, he defined the "great West" as the region of the continent occupied by westward-bound American and European pioneers who formed the "advancing frontier line" of the constantly expanding United States. But even Turner recognized that the West cannot be considered just a point on a map, but is the more elusive source of "perennial rebirth" that is so fundamental to United States history that it shapes "the forces dominating American character."

The American West is customarily defined as the country lying west of the Mississippi River and reaching to the Pacific Ocean, but this definition ignores the existence of earlier "Wests" and their continued influence on our contemporary world. Remarkably, from the nation's very earliest days there has been an American West. The western frontier was once located in what are now the eastern seaboard states, including New York. The current idea of the trans-Mississippi West as *the* West began around the time of Thomas Jefferson's 1803 Louisiana Purchase and Lewis and Clark's expedition the following year, through the vast, unexplored territory that extended from the Mississippi to the Rockies, and from the Gulf of Mexico to Canada. However, the idea of the West was formed long before then, in New York and other eastern states. If the Atlantic Ocean lapped at the eastern shores of the Colonies, an uncharted, seemingly limitless wilderness lapped at their western edges. Its vastness defied settlers' imaginations: it was more than three times the size of Europe. Nevertheless, English explorer John Cabot had claimed North America for England before 1500, and Captain John Smith, who helped found the permanent English settlement at Jamestown, Virginia, in 1607, had praised America as a paradise of endless abundance. Westward migration was inevitable. By the eighteenth century the West was an alluring destination; but its beckoning frontier, like a mirage, retreated constantly before the oncoming tide of the largest mass migration in history.

The virtual flood of artists who headed west did not gain momentum until after Lewis and Clark's expedition, which surprisingly did not include artists to document the territory's land, people, animals, and plants. However, artists were in the vanguard of western travelers. Beginning in the early 1800s, several adventurous explorer artists—notably George Catlin, John Mix Stanley, and Alfred Jacob Miller—made long journeys west, frequently up the two-thousand-mile-long Missouri River

7. Thomas Moran, *Clouds in the Canyon*, 1915. Oil on canvas, 20 x 25 inches. Gift of the Rockwell Foundation. 78.43

The future of American art lies in being true to our own country. . . . My chief desire is to call the attention of American landscape painters to . . . this enchanting southwestern country; a country flooded with color and picturesqueness, offering everything to inspire the artist.

—Thomas Moran, in *The Grand Canyon of Arizona,* 1909

into the heart of the Far West. They then returned to their eastern studios to paint the sights and events of the West based on their sketches and diaries. These images were instrumental in sparking the determination of Americans and others from around the world to plunge into the West's magnificence, excitement, and incomparable opportunities.

After the Mexican War of 1846, the Southwest became the newest territory of the United States. The federal government lost no time in sending scientific and military expeditions to explore and document this unique desert region, which had been populated for centuries by Hispanics and Mexicans, and for thousands of years by indigenous Indians. Fortunately, artists and photographers did go on these expeditions, charged with producing accurate documentary portrayals of significant southwestern landmarks. Like other "documentary" artists, Thomas Moran and William Henry Jackson called upon their gifts of observation, but also their Romantic tendencies, when they collaborated to produce stunning views of the Yellowstone region and the Grand Canyon.

Not all artists who went west during that period accompanied government or military expeditions. Samuel Colman and William de la Montagne Cary were among those who sought adventure on their own, while others went as illustrators for eastern magazines and publishing houses. N.C. Wyeth and his fellow artists from Howard Pyle's Brandywine School, near Chadd's Ford, Delaware, rendered thousands of vivid illustrations of the Old West, the Wild West, and the Far West for millions of eastern readers.

The escalation of the relentless, violent, and devastating Indian Wars, which from the 1860s to the early 1890s were fought largely on the Great Plains, attracted artists to the rugged and dangerous lives led by the U.S. Army soldiers and cowboys who became archetypal western heroes. Frederic Remington's and Charles Schreyvogel's scenes of military and cowboy life on the western frontier were hugely popular. Charlie Russell, who went to Montana as a youth, became the quintessential "cowboy artist."

Native Americans—and their cultures and customs—have been perennially favorite subjects for all kinds of artists. At the end of the nineteenth century, concerned artists vowed to capture "vanishing" American Indians on canvas or in bronze before their worlds were shattered by the force of westward expansion, renewing the alarm that George Catlin had sounded decades earlier. Joseph Henry Sharp made hundreds of sympathetic portraits of Indian leaders across the West that have great historic and aesthetic value. Artists working in the Southwest, including Ernest L. Blumenschein and his fellow members of the Taos Society of Artists, which was active between 1915 and 1927, usually portrayed placid Native Americans and Hispanics engaged in religious rituals or occupied by traditional daily tasks.

Artists still paint the traditional West in traditional styles, but during the past several decades many have turned to more subjective, even abstract interpretations of their experiences in the New West. Montana sculptor Deborah Butterfield creates semi-abstract horses from found materials to express elemental emotions, while New Mexico artist Jaune Quick-to-See Smith creates an aura of mystery and transcendence in her powerful paintings. Through their art, she and other Native American artists illuminate unique and vital views of the West.

Just as there is no one true West, there can be no one kind of western art. Artists in the West respond to the people, places, and ideas that have shaped and been shaped by the West. Through these linked, sometimes overlapping, themes we too can view the West in new ways not bounded by traditional notions. Most importantly, when considered as a dynamic gathering of people, places, and ideas, the West offers myriad meanings and an exciting and rewarding new appreciation of America, Americans, the American West, and American art.

Notes

1. Frederick Jackson Turner, "The Significance of the Frontier in American History," *Annual Report of the American Historical Association for 1893* (Washington, D. C.: GPO, 1894), 199–201.

Wilderness

8. Clyde Aspevig, *High Country Pond,* 1986. Oil on canvas, 32½ x 48¼ inches. Clara S. Peck Fund purchase. 86.23

Wilderness

The wilderness and the solitary place shall be glad for them; and the desert shall rejoice, and blossom as the rose.

—*Isaiah 35:1*

We are the land. . . . The Earth is the mind of the people as we are the mind of the earth. . . . The land is . . . as truly an integral aspect of our being as we are of its being.

—Paula Gunn Allen, in *The Remembered Earth*

All the pulses of the world,
Falling in they beat for us, with the Western movement beat,
Holding single or together, steady moving to the front, all for us,
Pioneers! O Pioneers!

—Walt Whitman, "Pioneers! O Pioneers!" in *Leaves of Grass*

THE TRADITIONAL TALE of western migration has been one of a preordained, inevitable expansion by eastern settlers into "the vacant wilderness of America."[1] In stark contrast to the idea that westward migration was the triumph of civilization against the wilderness (and, incidentally, its Native residents), for American Indians the catastrophic invasion of their world, popularly termed Manifest Destiny, had tragic consequences.

When viewed through the prisms of religious prophecy, economic need, political ambition, or simply the desire to begin life anew, adventurers and migrants gazing west toward its vast plains and rugged mountains saw a fantastic, pristine Eden—a New World Promised Land. For early pilgrims and later pioneers who believed they had a covenant with God to "tame" and cultivate "wild" America, it was vital to see the West as "wilderness."

This view collided head-on with the reality of the Native peoples who had occupied the West for millennia and for whom the land held

Howard Pyle and the Brandywine School of Artists

BY THE TIME prominent illustrator Howard Pyle (1853–1911) established his Brandywine School of American Illustration near Chadds Ford, Delaware, in 1898, dime novels and western movies were extremely popular. Artists including N.C. Wyeth, W.H.D. Koerner, Frank Schoonover, and Harvey Dunn studied with Pyle, who was more interested in stimulating their ability to illustrate stories imaginatively than in teaching painting techniques. According to Dunn's student John Clymer (who years earlier had been warned by Dunn that he was "too sickly" to be an illustrator), "It didn't matter how you put paint on a picture. It's what you had to say in the picture. How clearly you said it—how much you involved yourself with each person that was in your painting." (Goetzmann and Goetzmann, *The West of the Imagination,* 316.)

Several of Pyle's students, attracted to the West and seeking "total immersion" in their subject, traveled there and later became western illustrators. After his 1904 trip to what he lauded as "the great West," Wyeth wrote, "I felt reluctant to leave those brutal and rugged mountains, the dry, scorching plains. . . . The life is wonderful, strange—the fascination of it clutches me like some unseen animal—it seems to whisper, 'Come back, you belong here, this is your real home.'" (*Paintings of the Southwest,* 128) He returned west once again, in 1906, where he rode stagecoaches and visited Indian tribes. Wyeth produced more than four hundred illustrations based on his western adventures for most of the major magazines. Nevertheless, he finally settled with his artistically talented family at Chadd's Ford. The area soon became known as "Wyeth country."

Koerner, a German-born artist who grew up in the Midwest, also created hundreds of magazine illustrations featuring western subjects. He became most famous for *Madonna of the Prairie,* which he painted for the cover of *The Saturday Evening Post* in 1922 to illustrate Emerson Hough's serialized story, "The Covered Wagon." When it was made into a book, Koerner's *Madonna* was used on the book's dust jacket.

—S.C.

9. N. C. Wyeth, *I shall never forget the sight. It was like a great green sea*, 1918. Oil on canvas, 32 x 40 inches. Clara S. Peck Fund purchase. 94.9

10. John Clymer, *Time of Hunger*, 1975. Oil on canvas, 26 x 42 inches. Gift of Robert F. Rockwell, Jr. 78.405

profound ritual and cultural value. The seasonal, nomadic movement of many tribes across plains and through mountains, determined fundamentally by the cycles of the seasons, and the spiritual practices that had grown from them defined their wide-ranging world; for American Indians, the West that appeared pristine to strangers was neither wild nor empty, but *terra cognita*, familiar, beloved terrain. Even today, Native American artists such as Emmi Whitehorse relate to the so-called wilderness as intimate and elemental, as in her painting, *Water & Mineral* (Plate 19).

Clearly, the history of the American West, though it may appear to be "ostentatiously simple and monolithic," is in fact "a congeries of inner tensions"[2] based on cultural conflicts; in many ways the West and its history are still contested terrain. And yet, the romantic vision of the American wilderness, with its rugged, dangerous frontier, is still so deeply embedded in America's collective psyche that Americans have nicknamed Alaska the "last frontier," and space, the "final frontier."

Historically, artists of the American West have played significant roles in shaping how the world sees the West. In the nineteenth century, many of America's most prominent artists were imbued with the Romantic belief that the West offered ideal scenery for their canvases as well as fitting symbols of their own Americanness. Beyond even those lofty goals, many were determined to portray the West as the very soul of America, the fabulous symbol of its majesty and power. They were urged on by politicians and civic leaders; in the mid-1800s, a New York City magazine declared:

> The axe of civilization is busy with our old forests. . . . What were once the wild and picturesque haunts of the Red Man, and where the wild deer roamed in freedom, are becoming the abodes of commerce and the seats of manufactures. . . . It behooves our artists to rescue from its grasp the little that is left, before it is for ever too late.[3]

Landscape artists Albert Bierstadt and Thomas Moran eagerly accepted the challenge to paint "picturesque" western landmarks, for the sentiment expressed in the magazine coincided with their European art training and their goals as landscape painters. Steeped in the northern European Romantic tradition of portraying rugged mountains as haunts of the gods, they idealized their subjects in order to arrive at "higher truths."

11. William Robinson Leigh, *The Warning Shadow*, 1908. Gouache on paper, 27$\frac{1}{8}$ x 19$\frac{1}{4}$ inches. Gift of Sandra Rockwell Herron. 91.64

12. Carl Clemens Moritz Rungius, *In the Bighorn Country*, c. 1943. Oil on canvas, 28 x 90 inches. Museum purchase. 80.117

13. Carl Clemens Moritz Rungius, *Caribou (The Stranger)*, c. 1932. Oil on canvas, 30 x 45 inches. Gift of the Rockwell Foundation. 80.135

BORN IN BERLIN, Germany, in 1869, Carl Clemens Moritz Rungius was the grandson of a taxidermist and wild-game hunter. As a young boy Rungius, himself a hunter, took a serious interest in drawing the outdoors and animals. He had his first look at wild America when an uncle who lived in Brooklyn, New York, invited him along on a hunting trip to Maine in 1894. The following summer he hunted in Wyoming. Attracted by the landscape and plentiful game he discovered in the United States, he settled on Long Island, New York, in 1897, and spent summers hunting in the West. After a visit in 1910 to Alberta, Canada, he returned there every summer, claiming to be "in love" with the region. In 1921, he and his wife built a summer home and studio in Banff, which he christened "The Paint-

14. Carl Clemens Moritz Rungius, *Monarchs of the Wilderness*, c. 1901. Oil on canvas, 36 x 56 inches. Gift of the Rockwell Foundation. 78.437

box." He spent every summer there until 1958, a year before his death.

Rungius used vigorous brush strokes and dynamic color to capture the power, beauty, and drama of the western wilderness and its wildlife.

Specializing in painting big game such as mountain goats, caribou, moose, and sheep, he attracted the admiration of Theodore Roosevelt, noted for his own exploits as a big-game hunter. Rungius may have cast *Bull Moose* in bronze in 1905 in tribute to Roosevelt's "Bull Moose" Progressive Party. Roosevelt collected Rungius's work, whose authenticity reflects his years spent in the high country and forests of the American West, the Canadian Rockies, and the Yukon.

—S.C.

15. Norm Akers, *Elk Calling*, 1999. Oil on canvas, 66 x 60 inches. Clara S. Peck Fund purchase. 2000.17.1

Bierstadt, recently arrived in the West after painting the European Alps with fellow American artists Worthington Whittredge and Sanford Robinson Gifford, loved the Rocky Mountains. He aspired to capture the sublime in popular, monumental paintings such as *Mount Whitney* (Plate 17). One enthusiastic critic exclaimed that Bierstadt's paintings offered "a grand and gracious epitome and reflection of nature on this continent—of that majestic barrier of the West where the heavens and the earth meet in brilliant and barren proximity."[4]

Although Moran sought out inherently colorful and dramatic locales as the basis and inspiration for his paintings, he insisted that he placed "no value upon literal transcriptions of Nature. . . . All my tendencies are toward idealization. Of course, all art must come through Nature . . . but I believe that a place as a place, has . . . value . . . for the artist only so far as it furnishes the material from which to construct a picture."[5]

Next to Bierstadt, Thomas Hill was the best-known painter of California mountain scenery. Attracted to Yosemite, he settled nearby and painted it repeatedly, "not as it is, but as it ought to be." Similarly, Sydney Laurence, the first professional artist to settle in Alaska (in 1904) and the state's best-known painter, portrayed Mt. McKinley, his favorite subject, as a forbidding, wilderness stronghold (Plate 20).

Attracted by their aesthetic or narrative potential, or the spiritual beliefs they symbolize, some artists have chosen the wildlife of western America as their favorite subjects. Just as the buffalo has become the undisputed icon of the Great Plains, so these animals symbolize wild America as well as religious beliefs.

Native American and non-Native artists alike have trekked far into the back country of the United States and Canada to view these denizens of the wilds. Some, like Carl Rungius, have been avid big-game hunters. Others have captured their prey only in paint or bronze. Native American artists Norm Akers, in *Elk Calling* (Plate 15), and Mario Martinez, in *Yo Chiva`ato (Enchanted Goat)* (Plate 6), feature wild animals in mythical settings as expressions of spiritual and cultural values; their paintings are rich in layered meanings.

When William Robinson Leigh painted *The Warning Shadow* (Plate 11) in 1908, roles were reversed as the wary hunter became the mountain lion's intended prey. This illustration for a western story illuminates attitudes that were prevalent at the time about America's wild game. The popularity of big-game hunting was at its apex—President Theodore Roosevelt, himself an avid big-game hunter, decorated the White House with trophies he had taken in America, Asia, and Africa. Wild animals were valorized as dangerous but worthy adversaries for those who would tame the "wild" West.

John Clymer's more recent painting of a mountain lion stalking its unseen prey in *Time of Hunger* (Plate 10) places the lion in a wilderness setting where it can be admired for its beauty and cunning. Rungius also preferred to portray animals undisturbed in their natural habitat. An experienced outdoorsman, he spent much of his life packing into the remote reaches of North America to view the spectacular country and the magnificent animals he painted. Known as a wildlife artist, his landscapes frequently are as compelling as his animal portraits, as seen in *Caribou (The Stranger)* (Plate 13). Teddy Roosevelt was an enthusiastic fan and collector of Rungius's wildlife paintings, which he valued for their authenticity.

Like Rungius, Canadian Alexander Phimister Proctor tracked big game through the forests of western America from the time he was a youth. He devoted his career to sculpting large animals, inspired by Greek sculpture he considered "the pinnacle of perfection in sculptured

16. Alexander Proctor, *The Bull Moose*, 1903. Bronze, 18 1/4 x 16 x 9 inches. Gift of the Rockwell Foundation. 78.91

17. Albert Bierstadt, *Mount Whitney*, c. 1877. Oil on canvas, 68 7/8 x 116 5/8 inches. Gift of the Rockwell Foundation. 78.14

All men are in some degree impressed by the face of the world; some men even to delight. . . . Others have the same love in such excess, that, not content with admiring, they seek to embody it in new forms. The creation of beauty is Art.

—Ralph Waldo Emerson, *Nature*, 1836

18. Wilson Hurley, *La Cueva Cañon, Sandias*, 1982. Oil on canvas, 30 x 49 inches. Clara S. Peck Fund purchase. 86.22

The atmosphere of the Southwest is perhaps the hardest in the world for artists to catch. It is so subtle, so magical, so mixed with witchcraft, that it fools the sharpest eye and laughs at the cleverest palette.

—Charles F. Lummis, "The Artist's Paradise," *Out West*, September 1908

19. Emmi Whitehorse, *Water & Mineral*, January 2000. Oil chalk on paper on canvas, 40½ x 28 inches. Clara S. Peck Fund purchase. 2000.17.2

MY PAINTINGS TELL THE STORY of knowing the land over time—of being completely, microcosmically within a place. Luminous with the ambience of light and heat, they are purposefully meditative and are to be "seen slowly." My intricate language of symbols refers to specific plants, places, people, and experiences. These images float in and out of awareness.

—Emmi Whitehorse, artist's
statement, 1999

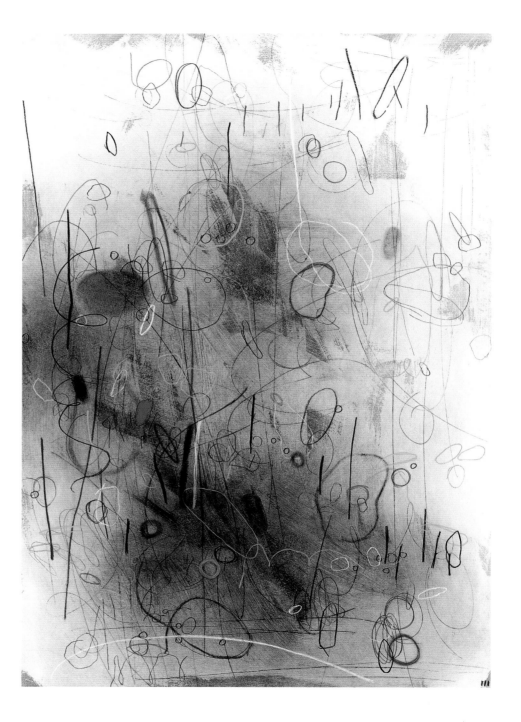

art." Western author J. Frank Dobie, who believed Proctor to be the greatest American wildlife sculptor, said that Proctor's work inspired in him "a kind of release and elation. I am free with them and with the wind, in spaces without confines."[6]

Winter in the West can be treacherous, especially for those not prepared to weather its extremes. In the nineteenth and early twentieth centuries, stories frequently came out of the West of immigrant parties reduced to cannibalism when they were stranded in the dead of winter by blizzards in isolated mountain passes; or of calamitous government expeditions, such as John C. Fremont's 1838 railway survey party, which was rumored to have resorted to cannibalism when it was lost in the snowbound mountains of northern New Mexico. For those who went west with the intention of "subduing wildernesses and savage tribes, felling forests, butchering buffaloes . . . , "[7] punishing conditions including freezing temperatures, deep snowdrifts, and scarce food were obstacles to be conquered. Frequently, as in Harvy Dunn's *Montana Winter Scene* (Plate 27), survival was a matter of man versus the elements.

Native Americans, too, faced winter's hardships—scarce game, scarcely adequate shelter, bone-chilling temperatures—but had developed successful strategies for accommodating their lives to the winter season. The complacent travelers in Henry Farny's painting, *On the Trail in Winter* (Plate 28), obviously are at home in the winter landscape they traverse. How different the mood of Dunn's frantic pioneers from that of the calm Indians, their stoic horses, and playful dogs as they ride comfortably along "the faint but traditionally grooved trails

20. Sydney Laurence, *Mount McKinley,* 1922. Oil on canvas, 53 x 43 inches. Gift of Gertrude Brewster. 80.36

Yosemite Valley

THE WALLS ARE MADE UP OF ROCKS, mountains in size . . . and they are so sheer in front, and so compactly and harmoniously arranged on a level floor, that the Valley . . . looks like an immense hall or temple lighted from above.

But no temple made with hands can compare with Yosemite. Every rock in its walls seems to glow with life. Some lean back in majestic repose; others . . . advance beyond their companions in thoughtful attitudes, giving welcome to storms and calms alike, seeming aware, yet heedless, of everything going on about them. Awful in stern, immovable majesty, how . . . fine and reassuring the company they keep; their feet among beautiful groves and meadows, their brows in the sky, a thousand flowers leaning confidingly against their feet, bathed in floods of water, floods of light, while the snow and waterfalls, the winds and avalanches and clouds shine and sing and wreathe about them as the years go by.

—John Muir, *The Yosemite*, 1912

21. Albert Bierstadt, *Yosemite Valley*, 1880. Oil on paper, mounted on canvas, 27½ x 20 inches. Gift of Robert F. Rockwell, Jr. 78.15

22. Thomas Hill, *Yosemite*, date unknown. Oil on canvas, 35⅝ x 29⅛ inches. Gift of the Rockwell Foundation. 85.56

23. John Mix Stanley, *The Smoke Signal,* 1868. Oil on canvas, 29⅝ x 22½ inches. Gift of the Rockwell Foundation. 78.68

that led them through their cycle."[8]

Because of its scarcity, water in the West is hugely important and highly valued. Thoughts of water in the West often concern its lack—Death Valley comes to mind, or nameless trackless deserts whose only water is a mirage, or Indian rain dances. In 1903, author Mary Austin, in her homage to the arid West in *The Land of Little Rain,* wrote, "Here are the long heavy winds and breathless calms on the tilted mesas where dust devils dance, whirling up into a wide, pale sky. Here you have no rain when all the earth cries for it, or quick downpours called cloud-bursts for violence. . . . The land sets its seasons by the rain."[9]

It is not surprising that western artists turn to water—in the form of rain, rivers, lakes, and even oceans—as subjects for their realistic landscapes and abstract expressions. In her ceramic vessel *Rain Bird* (Plate 26), Christine McHorse created a reverential sculpture that celebrates the precious element, literally in the form of rain; the work itself is shiny and shaped like a raindrop. The tantalizingly remote lakes pictured in Clyde Aspevig's *High Country Pond* (Plate 8) and Ogden Pleissner's *Lost Lake, Wyoming* (Plate 29) are reposeful jewels inviting meditation and renewal.

In the twentieth century, artists were confronted with the New West and relics of what might be called the Failed West, for westward expansion often left in its wake no landmark more durable than the ample evidence of failed dreams. In *Old West, Bagdad Siding—Mohave Desert* (Plate 30), photographer David De Harport captured the melancholy that pervades much of today's West. But even in this graphic depiction of decay and the death of dreams, a bit of the romance of the West lingers on, if only in the exotic name of the abandoned railway stop.

24. Thomas Moran, *Green River*, 1877. Oil on canvas, 10 x 16 $^{11}/_{16}$ inches. Clara S. Peck bequest. 83.46.14

GREEN RIVER was the first subject that Thomas Moran sketched in the West. He discovered the fabulously dramatic site in 1871 while on his way to join Ferdinand V. Hayden's U.S. Geological and Geographical Survey expedition to the Yellowstone country as its official artist. A Union Pacific Railroad terminal was near the place where craggy towers, sheer cliffs, and the placid river were joined, in Green River, Wyoming, but Moran never included it or even indicated that it was nearby. Rather, he painted the Green River area as unexplored territory; the group of riders that he usually painted into the scene added a highly romantic dimension to the already fantastic landscape. This Green River location would remain a favorite subject for Moran, who made scores of paintings and sketches, each a slightly different study during the next thirty years.

Influenced by the emotionally charged, atmospheric paintings of the English painter J. M. W. Turner, Moran's use of luminous, transparent paint in rich oranges, pinks, azures, and golds came to typify his western paintings.

—*S.C.*

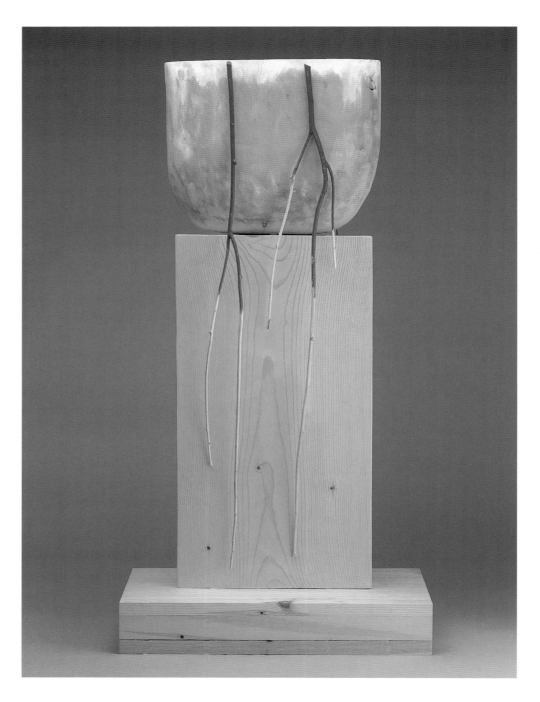

25. Truman Lowe, *Feather Basket*, 1999. Wood and paint, 31 x 13½ x 10 inches. Clara S. Peck Fund purchase. 2000.35

Beauty in simplicity is the basis for my work in clay and silver. The shiny earth and metal provide personal means of expression through the oldest crafts.

—Christine McHorse, 1998, in
St. James Guide to Native North American Artists

26.   Christine McHorse, *Rain Bird*, 1999. Micaceous clay, 11½ x 10 inches diameter. Clara S. Peck Fund purchase. 2000.28.1

27. Harvey Thomas Dunn, *Montana Winter Scene*, 1907. Oil on canvas, 36¼ x 24 inches. Gift of James McMahon. 78.107

HARVEY DUNN (1884–1952) was born in South Dakota but went east to join the Brandywine group of illustrators at Chadds Ford, Delaware. He, like N.C. Wyeth, Frank Schoonover, and several other artists who gathered there, became a devotee of western illustration. Unlike them, however, he did not illustrate "cowboys and shoot-'em-ups." His favorite subjects were western farmers and pioneers, partly in tribute to his father, a Dakota "sod-buster." As a leading illustrator for *The Saturday Evening Post*, he was noted for his "imaginative compositions that threaded their way through the text . . . turning the printed sheet itself into a visual adventure. . . . He thrived on the challenge of layout and design posed by the magazine work." (Goetzmann and Goetzmann, *The West of the Imagination*)

—S.C.

28. Henry Farny, *On the Trail in Winter*, 1894. Gouache on paper, 15¾ x 10⅞ inches. Gift of the Rockwell Foundation. 78.31

—— THE AMERICAN WEST ——

30. David De Harport, *The Old West, Bagdad Siding—Mohave Desert*, 1964 negative/1984 print. Silver selenium print, 11 x 14 inches. Gift of the artist. 87.5

Buffalo

31. William Robinson Leigh, *The Buffalo Hunt*, 1947. Oil on canvas, 78 x 126 ¼ inches. Gift of the Rockwell Foundation. 78.37

AT LAST THE DAY CAME when my father allowed me to go on a buffalo hunt with him. And what a proud boy I was! Ever since I could remember my father had been teaching me the things that I should know and preparing me to be a good hunter. . . . I knew how to ride my pony no matter how fast he would go, and I felt that I was brave and did not fear danger. All these things I had learned for just this day when father would allow me to go with him on a buffalo hunt. It was the event for which every Sioux boy eagerly waited.

—Luther Standing Bear, *My Indian Boyhood*, 1931, in Valerius Geist, *Buffalo Nation: History and Legend of the North American Bison*

Buffalo

The buffalo was part of us. . . . It was hard to say where the animal ended and the man began.

—John Fire Lame Deer, *Lame Deer, Seeker of Visions*

The civilization of the Indian is impossible while the buffalo remains upon the plains.

—Columbus Delano, U.S. Secretary of Interior, 1873

AT THE TURN OF THE CENTURY, when prominent sculptor James Earle Fraser sought "truly American" symbols for his design of a coin for the U.S. Treasury, he concluded that none was "so distinctive as the American buffalo." Ironically, Fraser's buffalo nickel appeared when the North American buffalo, *Bison bison,* was nearly extinct and efforts to protect and conserve the remaining small herds were ineffectual.

Spanish explorers in the Southwest were the first Europeans to encounter buffalo. In 1542, Francisco Vasquez de Coronado, astonished by the sheer number his party had sighted on the western plains, reported that their horses "took flight on seeing them, for they are horrible to the sight." During the Lewis and Clark expedition through the trans-Mississippi West, Lewis noted in his journal that they had spotted more buffalo than they "had ever seen before at one time; and if it be not impossible to calculate the moving multitude, which darkened the whole plains, we are convinced that twenty thousand would be no exaggerated number." In fact the North American buffalo once numbered up to sixty million.

Most Native American creation stories agree that the first buffalo emerged from a hole or cave, usually in the side of a mountain. Crow Chief Plenty Coups told his biographer the Crow story that, "Out of the hole in the ground came the buffalo, bulls and cows and calves without number. They spread wide and blackened the plains."

In mere decades after Americans appeared on the plains, these herds were decimated. By the early 1830s, few if any buffalo could be found east of the Mississippi River; between 1830 and 1870 the buffalo population had dropped to a few million. As early as 1842, artist George Catlin wrote that the buffalo had "recently fled before the appalling appearance of civilized man." He predicted that "its species is soon to be extinguished, and with it the peace and happiness (if not the actual existence) of the tribes of Indians who are joint tenants with them, in the occupancy of these vast and idle plains."

Nevertheless, by the 1880s, as settlers pushed west in ever-growing numbers, the federal government mounted a concerted campaign to exterminate the remaining buffalo in order to drive the Indians who depended on them onto reservations, opening the West for settlement.

32. Henry Merwin Shrady, *Elk Buffalo (Monarch of the Plains)*, 1901. Bronze, 23 x 32 x 12 inches. Museum purchase. 78.943

The Kiowas were camped on the north side of Mount Scott, those of them who were still free to camp. One young woman got up very early in the morning. The dawn mist was still rising from Medicine Creek, and as she looked across the water, peering through the haze, she saw the last buffalo appear like a spirit dream.

Straight to Mount Scott the leader of the herd walked. Behind him came the cows and their calves, and the few young males who had survived. As the woman watched, the face of the mountain opened.

Inside Mount Scott the world was green and fresh, as it had

been when she was a small girl. The rivers ran clear, not red. The wild plums were in blossom. . . . Into this world of beauty the buffalo walked, never to be seen again.

—Folk tale as told by Old Lady Horse (Kiowa) [6]

33. Norman Rockwell, *The Buffalo Hunt*, c. 1914–1915. Oil on canvas, 20 x 32 inches. Gift of Robert F. Rockwell III. 78.52

By the turn of the twentieth century, no more than a few hundred buffalo still survived. Hunkpapa Sioux Chief Sitting Bull lamented, "A cold wind blew across the prairie when the last buffalo

34. Charles Marion Russell, *A Game Country*, March 4, 1917. Illustrated letter on paper, 11 x 8½ inches. Gift of the Rockwell Foundation. 85.63

CHARLIE RUSSELL, who corresponded with a wide circle of friends and acquaintances, is almost as well known for his illustrated letters as he is for his western paintings and sculpture. With a record of "poor academic achievement," his letters' grammar, punctuation, and "idiosyncratic" spelling are colorful if not correct. As early as 1903, letters to friends in his hometown of Saint Louis, "such as Bill Rance at the Silver Dollar, were not only posted near the bar for all to see but published in the newspaper as well."

In 1929, Russell's widow, Nancy Russell, published his letters in a volume titled *Good Medicine*, with an introduction by Will Rogers. In his inscription to Nancy in the first numbered copy of the book, Rogers wrote, "He didn't know he was writing for all the ages did he. He left us Nancy, but he left us much." (Peter Hassrick, *Charles M. Russell*)

—S.C

C. M. RUSSELL
GREAT FALLS, MONTANA

March 4 1917

My Dear Mr Shaw

I did not get your letter till I reached home but I thank you and Mr Lindsley for the kind invitation and if that invite holds good I may visit him som other time maby next year I would like to have one more look at a game country before they turn the parke in to a sheep range and they geysers to a steam laundrey theirs an aufall wast of hot water in the Yellowstone park enough to wash in side and out all the reformers in the state and theirs a fiew of them

thanking you again and if you ever cross my range the latch strings out

C M Russell

35. Joseph Henry Sharp, *Prayer to the Spirit of the Buffalo*, 1910. Oil on canvas, 30 x 40 inches. Gift of the Rockwell Foundation. 78.63

it is not the words of the chant
that make the prayer
it is the way they are said
that reaches gods ear

—from Norman H. Russell, "The Words,"
in *The Remembered Earth*

36. Artist(s) unknown (Dakota) Painted Buffalo Hide Robe, c. 1883. Buffalo hide, pigments, 82 x 69 inches. Museum purchase. 78.104.1

In this early example of painting by Plains Indians, an exquisitely painted buffalo hide contains several likely interpretations of feather war bonnets. These geometric patterns and designs reflect a sophisticated exploration of line, rhythm and balance, just as well-designed feathered bonnets do in three dimensions. Traditionally women in Plains cultures painted geometric designs and men specialized in narrative, representational imagery. However, the similarity between the depiction of war bonnets in clearly male-authored ledger drawings and the war bonnets transformed into design on this hide defy these simple gender divisions.

—*K.E.A.*

fell . . . a death-wind for my people." Some dismissed the prolonged massacre as a matter of "survival of the fittest," but many other citizens, alarmed by the slaughter, publicized the buffalos' plight. As Henry Merwin Shrady did in his sculpture, *Elk Buffalo (Monarch of the Plains)* (Plate 32), many artists memorialized the vanished buffalo.

Also in a nostalgic vein, the youthful Norman Rockwell captured the intense drama of an Indian buffalo hunt in his dynamic 1915 *Buffalo Hunt* (Plate 33). In the large 1947 painting, *The Buffalo Hunt* (Plate 31), William Robinson Leigh portrayed Indians hunting buffalo on horseback while also engaging in the archaic if visually dramatic practice of driving buffalo over a "jump," a hunting technique abandoned after horses arrived on the plains in the 1500s.

Rather than glorify the hunt, Joseph Henry Sharp focused on the devastating impact the demise of the buffalo had on Indian culture in his subtle and sensitive portrait, *Prayer to the Spirit of the Buffalo* (Plate 35). Prayers may have been answered, for buffalo are returning to the West. Several tribes have reestablished herds on their lands. The federal government has reintroduced buffalo into national parks. Artists of the late 1800s and early 1900s memorialized the departed buffalo; today, artists forecast the return of buffalo like those thundering across the heavens in Rosalie Favell's *Navigating by Our Grandmothers* (Plate 90).

Have the spirits let us down? Listen to the prophecies! . . .The buffalo are returning. . . . Fences can't hold them. Irrigation water for the Great Plains is disappearing, and so are the farmers, and their plows. Farmers' children retreat to the cities. Year by year the range of the buffalo grows a mile or two larger.

—Leslie Marmon Silko, *Almanac of the Dead*, 1991

Notes

1. Valerius Geist, *Buffalo Nation: History and Legend of the North American Bison* (Stillwater, MN: Voyageur Press, 1996), 8.

2. *Buffalo Nation*, 59.

3. Meriwether Lewis, 1806, in *Buffalo Nation*, 63.

4. Crow Chief Plenty-coups, in Frank Bird Linderman, *American: The Life Story of a Great Indian, Plenty-coups, Chief of the Crows* (New York: The John Day Company, Inc., 1930), no page.

5. George Catlin, *Letters and Notes on the Manners, Customs, and Condition of the North American Indians*, 1842 , no page.

6. Wolf Calf (Piegan), in Peter Nabokov, ed., *Native American Testimony: A Chronicle of Indian-White Relations From Prophecy to the Present, 1492–1992* (New York: Viking, 1978, 1991), 43.

7. Hunkpapa Sioux Chief Sitting Bull, in *Buffalo Nation*, 101.

Horses

37. William de la Montagne Cary, *Indians Jousting*, c. 1875. Oil on canvas, 5¾ x 10⅝ inches. Gift of Sandra Rockwell Herron. 78.21

Horses . . .

Oh, how we used to love drawing horses. Even before we could write, all the young boys would gather around to see who could out-draw the other: horses that ran full tilt; horses that gathered at the watering hole; horses that threw their riders . . .

—Gerald McMaster, *Mistatim, The Horse of My Memory*

IMAGINE THE WEST WITHOUT HORSES: swift ponies, cavalry steeds, stagecoach teams. Pack animals. Spirit guides, wild mustangs. Racers, jumpers, rodeo broncs. Dude ranch nags. Cowboys' companions.

The buffalo may be the undisputed icon of the American West, but the horse has become the abiding icon of Western culture. In the West, as elsewhere in the world, horses were vital to virtually all human enterprise well into the twentieth century. In today's West, where horses are status symbols, playthings, and pets, most "horses" power automobiles, and it's train locomotives, not animals, that are "iron horses" (*Iron Horse*, Plate 48).

> They described the Fast Wagon as a big black horse with his belly nearly touching the ground. This horse had a big bell on his back. He ran so fast that every time he stopped, he puffed.
>
> —Plenty Coups (Crow), 1880s, *Native American Testimony*

Horses were not indigenous neighbors of the buffalo and Indians on the Great Plains. They arrived in North America in the mid-1500s with Francisco Vasquez de Coronado, who led his *conquistadores* north from Mexico in a quest for gold, taking as many as one thousand horses

38. Deborah Butterfield, Untitled, 2000.
Unique bronze, 45 x 56 x 16 inches. Clara S.
Peck Fund purchase. 2000.15

onto the plains. It is difficult to imagine Native Americans' reactions when they first saw horses, especially riders on horseback. More than one hundred years ago, Wolf Calf told the story of his tribe's first contact with horses: "All the Piegans were astonished and wondered what this could be. None of them had ever seen anything like it, and they were afraid. . . . The chief of the Piegans called out to his people: 'This is something very strange. I have heard of wonderful things that have happened . . . but I never heard of anything like this. This thing must have come from above, or else it must have come out of the hill.'" [1]

The advent of the horse changed life rapidly—and radically—for most Native Americans. In just a few decades horses transformed concepts of time and space. Social customs—from warfare to travel and migration, hunting, sports, and religious practice—were altered irrevocably. By the early 1700s, Native America had entered into what is termed the Horse Culture period, which lasted until the late 1800s when buffalo herds were diminished and Indian nations defeated.

Horses have been an integral part of life nearly everywhere in the world, and even now remain a universal subject for artists. In the West, the sight of wild horses and Indians riding horses captivated early artists. George Catlin, fascinated with "the wild horses, which are found in great numbers on the prairies," illustrated Indians taming them (*Breaking Down the Wild Horse*, Plates 40, 41, and 42) and described the technique: "They are taken with the laso, which is a long halter or thong, made of raw-hide. . . . and which the Indians throw with great dexterity, with a noose at one end of it, which drops over the head of the animal. . . . the Indian dismounts from his own horse, and holding to the end of the laso, choaks the animal down, and afterwards tames and converts him to his own use."[2]

Decades later, Cyrus Dallin made his reputation as a sculptor of Native Americans and equestrian figures, which he combined elegantly in works like *On the Warpath* (Plate 39). Until Dallin successfully exhibited his sculptures of Native Americans, equestrian statues usually honored U.S. Army war heroes. Dallin adopted the heroic, neoclassical style that was in vogue in Paris when he studied there in the late 1880s. And it was in Paris, not the American West, that he saw Buffalo Bill's Wild West show and decided to make his subjects the horses and Native Americans of the West.

Coastal California is not generally considered the Wild West, or the

39. Cyrus Dallin, *On the Warpath*, 1914. Bronze, 41¾ x 41 x 13 inches. Clara S. Peck Fund purchase. 95.11

40. George Catlin, *Breaking Down the Wild Horse*, c. 1830s. Oil on canvas, 26 x 32 inches. Clara S. Peck bequest. 83.46.25

41. George Catlin, *Breaking Down the Wild Horse*, from *North American Indian Portfolio*, c. 1844–1848. Hand-colored lithograph, 12¼ x 17⅞ inches. Clara S. Peck Fund purchase. 2000.19

IN HIS EXTENSIVE TRAVELS through the West, from the Mississippi to the Pacific and Alaska to Tierra del Fuego, Catlin created the most comprehensive record in the existance of the Native peopls of the vast region. A romantic, he tended to exaggerate or alter subjects and scenes. For instance, he painted landscapes in unnatural green hues to reflect his view of the American Wet as "the great and almost boundless garden spot of the earth, over whose green enamelled fields . . . Nature's proudest, noblest men have pranced on their wild horses." Still, Catlin's paintings and journals, which he published in his massive *Letters and Notes on the Manners, Customs, and Conditions of the North American Indians* (1841), are considered generally reliable.

Like many wetern artists, Catlin returned again and again to a successful subject, rendering it in many mediums. Lithography allowed him to distribute his images widely and provided an important source of income. While recognizable as the same subject, the distinctive qualities of each medium create interesting variations.

—S.C.

42. George Catlin, *Breaking Down the Wild Horse*, c. 1840. Graphite and white wash on paper, 12 x 17¾ inches. Clara S. Peck Fund purchase. 86.10

43. Alfred Jacob Miller, *Crow Chief on the Lookout*, c. 1840. Oil on canvas, 11½ x 9¾ inches. Clara S. Peck bequest. 83.46.11

A MAGNIFICENT MILK-WHITE charger, large-eyed, small-headed, bluff-chested, and with the dignity of a thousand monarchs in his lofty, overscorning carriage. He was the elected Xerxes of vast herds of wild horses, whose pastures in those days were only fenced by the Rocky Mountains and the Alleghenies. . . . The flashing cascade of his mane, the curving comet of his tail, invested him with housings more resplendent than gold and silver-beaters could have furnished him. A most imperial and archangelical apparition of that unfallen, western world. . . in whatever aspect he presented himself, always to the bravest Indians he was the object of trembling reverence and awe.

—Herman Melville,
Moby Dick or The Whale, 1851

Old West; only marginally is it considered the Far West. But it was there, where Spanish mission life, Mexican vaqueros and American cowboys, Native Americans, and longhorn cattle composed a distinctive variation on the theme of the West, that Edward Borein was born. His hometown, San Leandro, was on a cattle trail, and as a boy Borein sketched the cowboys, longhorn cattle, and horses that would continue to attract him. Like his friend Charlie Russell, Borein gave up formal art training to become a cowboy but sketched cowboy life throughout his entire career, even after the California West that he loved disappeared around the turn of the century, as rangeland was fenced in and Indians were confined on reservations by the U.S. government. *The Passing Herd* or *Cattle and Horsemen* (Plate 65) is Borein's nostalgic homage to those days.

In his paintings of horses, Charlie Russell captured the essence of rough-and-tumble cowboy life on the western range: horses throwing their riders, tangling with wild-eyed cattle, generally creating mayhem, as in *A Mix Up* (Plate 71) and *One Down, Two to Go* (Plate 70). Frederic Remington examined horse anatomy and locomotion in Eadweard Muybridge's 1882 volume, *Animal Locomotion*. Horses were so central to his art that he confided to a friend that he wanted his epitaph to be, "He knew the horse." *The Bronco Buster* (Plate 61) was Remington's first and one of his most popular sculptures—more than two hundred were cast in bronze. The piece was technically ambitious—the horse reared on

44. Frederic Remington, *The Cheyenne*, 1901. Bronze (ed. 40), 19¾ x 23 x 9 inches. Gift of the Rockwell Foundation. 78.93

45. Carl F. Wimar, *On the Warpath*, 1860. Oil on canvas, 6½ x 9⅜ inches. Clara S. Peck bequest. 83.46.8

46. Delbert Buck, *Bull Rider with Sheep*, date unknown, wood, fabric, pigment, 15 x 12 x 5 inches; *Chicken Rider*, date unknown, wood, fabric, pigment, 15 x 15 x 5 inches; *Cowboy on Zebra*, date unknown, wood, fabric, pigment 15 x 16 x 4 inches. Mamie Deschillie, untitled, date unknown, cardboard, fabric, pigment, sequins, 13 x 9 x 2 inches; untitled, date unknown, cardboard, paper, fabric, pigment, 13 x 9 x 2 inches. Museum purchase. 2000.20.1-5.

NAVAJO FOLK ART skirts the line between fine art and craft. Mamie Deschillie, a Navajo matriarch, and Delbert Buck, a young artist from a family of craftspeople, both have found success in this growing area of the contemporary art market. Although Navajos are documented as creating "mud toys" as early as the nineteenth century, art made by self-taught artists from such materials as cardboard, fabric, sequins, unfired clay, and wood carving has only recently been recognized by the mainstream art world. The work is often imaginative and whimsical, and typically figurative in nature, featuring such subjects as horses, sheep, buffalo, birds, and Navajo people in both traditional and contemporary dress, as well rodeo riders and cars.

—*K. E. A.*

47. Michael Eastman, *Horse #2*, 1999. Iris/Giclee print (1/23), 18 x 18 inches. Clara S. Peck Fund purchase. 99.20

48. Carm Little Turtle, *Iron Horse*, 1990/2000. Sepia toned photograph with oils, 8 x 12½ inches. Clara S. Peck Fund purchase. 2000.39

Notes

1. Wolf Calf (Piegan), in Peter Nabokov, ed., *Native American Testimony: A Chronicle of Indian-White Relations From Prophecy to the Present, 1492–1992* (New York: Viking, 1978, 1991), 43.

2. George Catlin, *Letters and Notes on the Manners, Customs and Conditions of North American Indians*, in *Heritage: The Magazine of the New York State Historical Association* (vol. 13, nos. 3–4, Spring/Summer 1997), 41.

3. William H. Goetzmann and William N. Goetzmann, *The West of the Imagination* (New York: W.W. Norton & Company, 1986), 247.

4. *Century Magazine*, June 1896, in Wayne Craven, *Sculpture in America* (New York: Thomas Y. Crowell Company, 1968), 534.

5. *West of the Imagination*, 247.

its hind legs—and Remington admitted that it was made with "great difficulties on my part." Critics came to consider his bronze horses with riders a "kind of western American version of the mythical centaur."

Horse culture in the West may have ended abruptly at the turn of the twentieth century, as trains and automobiles became more efficient modes of transportation, but the horse still rides in the West of our imaginations, and in art of the West. Montana sculptor Deborah Butterfield has devoted her career to horses, both in art and in her "engagement with learning and training horses and being trained by horses." For her, the image of the horse "evokes, in subtle ways," life's experiences (Plate 38). The splendid horse's head in Michael Eastman's *Horse #2* (Plate 47) brings art of the horse full circle; the closeup reveals only the horse's head in a profile that would be at home on an ancient Roman coin. In the art of the West the horse has become timeless symbol.

and Indians . . .

49. Seth Eastman, *The Tanner*, 1848. Oil on canvas, 30½ x 25¼ inches. Gift of Robert F. Rockwell, Jr. 78.29

and Indians . . .

*It makes little difference. . .where one opens the record of the history of the
Indians; every page and every year has its dark stain. The story of one tribe
is the story of all, varied only by differences of time and place.*

—Helen Hunt Jackson, *A Century of Dishonor*, 1881

. . .it is together—
all of us remembering what we have heard together—
that creates the whole story
the long story of the people.

—Leslie Marmon Silko, *Storyteller*, 1981

LIKE MUCH OF WESTERN HISTORY, from the beginning art of the American West has centered on Indians. It was the presence of Native Americans in the West that drew the earliest artists into its magnificent forests, plains, mountains, and deserts, and Native Americans who have held center stage—if few speaking roles—since that time.

In the 1830s, George Catlin headed west with an extremely ambitious mission: to paint the customs, cultures, and portraits of the Indians of North America. He eventually traveled the entire western hemisphere, from Alaska to Tierra del Fuego, his determination fueled by his conviction that Indians were "rapidly passing away from the face of the earth."

In 1832 he went up the Missouri River on the maiden voyage of the steamboat *Yellowstone*, and spent a great deal of time with the Mandan Indians who lived along the river, painting more than one hundred and fifty portraits and scenes of Mandan life (*Mandan Indians*, Plate 55). In 1867, he published an account of Mandan religious rituals.

By 1840 Catlin boasted that he had visited forty-eight tribes and from his sketches had painted more than three hundred portraits in oil, "also 200 other paintings in oil containing views of their villages . . . their games and religious ceremonies . . . their buffalo hunting and other

50. Rick Bartow, *Dog, Deer, and Me*, 1996.
Pastel, charcoal, graphite on paper, 40 x 26
inches. Clara S. Peck Fund purchase.
2000.25.2

sometimes

   i dream

of a place

   where you

can whisper

   with the wind

     —Maurice Kenny,
"shaman star dancer,"
in *Remembered Earth*

51. Henry Farny, *The Wailer*, 1895. Gouache on paper, 9 1/8 x 14 3/4 inches. Gift of Robert F. Rockwell, Jr. 78.3

I see, far in the west . . . a limitless ravine,
with plains and mountains dark,
I see swarms of stalwart chieftains,
medicine-men, and warriors,
As flitting by like clouds of ghosts, they pass and
are gone in the twilight . . .

—Walt Whitman, "Pioneers! O Pioneers!" in *Leaves of Grass*

52. Allan Houser/Haozous, *Apache Gans Dancer*, 1980. Bronze (lifetime cast, ed. 7/12), 28 x 9 x 12 inches. Clara S. Peck Fund purchase. 2000.38

amusements" as well as landscapes. Catlin exhibited hundreds of paintings and drawings in his traveling "Indian Gallery." In 1841, he published the two-volume book *Letters and Notes on the Manners, Customs, and Conditions of the North American Indians*, illustrated with line engravings of his paintings. Inspired by Catlin's Indian Gallery, John Mix Stanley went west to paint Indians for a gallery of his own. In 1865, his gallery was destroyed in a disastrous fire at the Smithsonian Institution where it was on loan. Tragically, it was only the first of three fires that destroyed nearly all of his work. In surviving paintings including *The Smoke Signal* (Plate 23), painted in 1868, Stanley posed his subjects heroically on rocky outcroppings.

When the early white artists penetrated beyond the Mississippi and up the Missouri, they found a cultural panoply that almost beggared their craft. . . . Still, . . . these artists—Catlin, Bodmer, Miller, Bierstadt—got down the true, vibrant variety of the Plains culture before it was reduced to the caricature of the war bonnet and the blanket.

—Frederick Turner, *Beyond Geography: The Western Spirit Against the Wilderness*, 1980

Catlin, Bodmer, Bierstadt, and Miller were among the first, but were hardly the last, artists to travel up the Missouri River; for decades, the journey was a rite of passage for artists who wanted to paint the land and native peoples of the West. Henry Farny became interested in painting Indians in 1881. He headed up the Missouri, sketching, taking notes, and collecting Indian artifacts, the first of many trips he made in the West. His paintings reveal that his sympathies clearly were with the dignified Native Americans he portrayed (*On the Trail in Winter*, Plate 28, and *The Wailer*, Plate 51).

When the Indian Wars escalated in the late 1800s, Indians were no longer portrayed as denizens of an undisturbed wilderness, but as savage warriors—the "hostiles" fought by the United States Cavalry as America's Manifest Destiny pushed settlers across the plains to the Pacific. Illustrators chose battles, skirmishes, and confrontations with Indians as favorite subjects in works such as William H.D. Koerner's *Tomahawk and Long Rifle* (Plate 54). By the close of the Wars, in the early 1890s, many artists were once again alarmed by the prospect that Indians were vanishing from the West. They portrayed them as the last of a dying

53. Cyrus Dallin, *Archery Lesson*, 1907. Bronze, 19 x 11 x 7 inches. Gift of Robert F. Rockwell III. 94.1

54. William H. D. Koerner, *Tomahawk and Long Rifle*, 1928. Oil on canvas, 27½ x 39⅝ inches. Gift of Robert F. Rockwell III. 78.36

"Ask him," instructed the hunter, who knew little of the Blackfeet language, "just why he enters the stockade armed." This illustration, along with this caption, was one of several that Koerner produced for Stewart Edward White's serialized story, "The Long Rifle," which ran in *The Saturday Evening Post* in 1931.

55. George Catlin, *Mandan Indians*, 1871. Oil on paper, mounted on canvas, 18 x 24½ inches. Gift of the Rockwell Foundation. 78.23

...AFTER THE FIRES were made I set my self down with the bigwhite man Chiefe [Bigwhite (Sheheke), a Mandan Chief who traveled with Lewis and Clark] and made a number of enquiries into the tredition of his nation. . . . He told me his nation first came out of the ground where they had a great village.

A grape vine grew down through the Earth to their village and they Saw light Some of their people ascended by the grape vine upon the earth, and saw Buffalow and every kind of animal also Grapes plumbs &c. . . . and deturmined to go up and live upon earth, and great numbers climbed the vine and got

upon earth men womin and children. at length a large big bellied woman in climbing broke the vine and fell and all that were left in the village below has remained there ever since.

—William Clark, *Journals of the Lewis and Clark Expedition*, August 18, 1806

56. Diego Romero, *Never Forget: Jim Thorpe, All-American*, 2000. Ceramic, polychrome, gilt, 18 x 10 inches diameter. Clara S. Peck Fund purchase. 2000.28.3.a-b

Andy Warhol
$ power
fame position
yer teacher
competition bia
rocknroll alcohol
drugs grades school
yer teachers job
a new car new stereo
live amerikan
sell amerikan
talk amerikan
die amerikan

sacred pipe ` sacred tobacco
sweat lodge round dance
animal/teachers
plants/medicines
tree of peace
language of dreams
smiles of drum, song, flute
grandparents
children
sundance kiva medicine people
prophecies teachings
earth lodge skin lodge wood lodge

turn my eyeholes to face the east

—Karoniaktatie (Alex Jacobs),
in *The Remembered Earth*

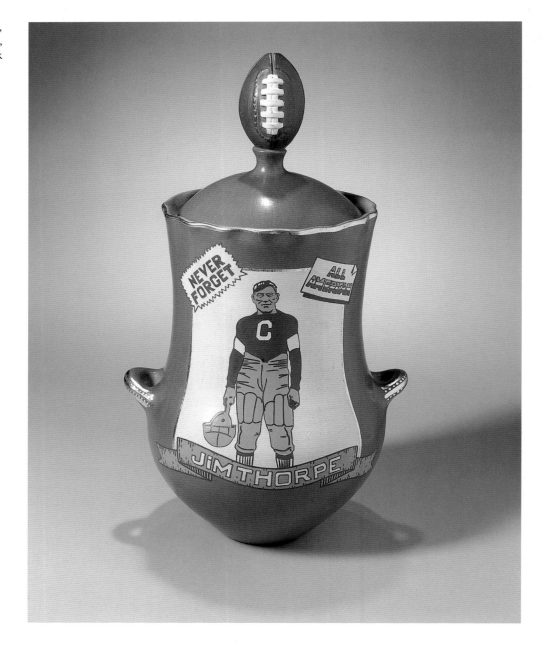

WORTHINGTON WHITTREDGE studied in Dusseldorf with Emmanuel Leutze, who also taught Albert Bierstadt. Whittredge traveled with Bierstadt through the Swiss Alps in 1857, but he was more interested in creating intimate, quiet paintings of Native peoples than the grand, theatrical compositions for which Bierstadt became famous.

In the mid-1860s, Whittredge accompanied General John Pope's party on an inspection tour of Missouri Territory. Known as a painter of eastern landscapes, after this western excursion Whittredge also painted the Great Plains, which he considered "Arcadian."

—*S.C.*

57. Worthington Whittredge, *Arapaho Lodge*, c. 1870. Oil on paper mounted on board, 11 3/8 x 10 5/8 inches. Acquired with proceeds of the Chili and Chocolate Roundup (1991), 91.62

race, as in Joseph H. Sharp's symbolic *Prayer to the Spirit of the Buffalo* (Plate 35). Farny's 1895 painting, *The Wailer* (Plate 51), depicts an Indian mourning the death of a comrade who is laid out on the bier in the background; but it also can be seen as a more general lament for "vanishing" Indians.

> We live on haunted land, on land that is layers deep in human passion and memory. . . . In truth, the tragedies of the wars are our national joint property, and how we handle that property is one test of our unity or disunity, maturity or immaturity, as people wearing the label "American."
>
> —Patricia Nelson Limerick, *Something In the Soil: Field-testing the New Western History*, 2000

Through the centuries of American experience in the West, Indians have been the subjects of non-Native artists. At the same time, Native American artists have produced a rich variety of works which reflect Native views of themselves, their cultures, and their lands. Historically, Native American art has been important to artists and scholars of the West, usually as the source of accurate detail in costumes, weapons, tipis, utensils, and religious artifacts. Native American art also has affected the work of non-Native artists directly, by inspiring color schemes, compositions, and perspectives. It also has been the subject of still life paintings.

It wasn't until the 1920s that Native American art began to be appreciated by non-Natives, and then usually in the art centers of Santa Fe and New York City. Liberal modernist artists and avant-garde intellectuals promoted and encouraged revivals of traditional art forms. In the 1930s, Allan Houser/Haozous studied art in two federally-sponsored art programs in Santa Fe, New Mexico, and Fort Sill, Oklahoma. After mastering the so-called traditional techniques and styles taught in these institutions, he developed his own artistic voice in order to portray his Chiricahua Apache people (*Apache Gans Dancer*, Plate 52) based on

58. Andy Warhol, *Geronimo*, 1986. Silkscreen on paper (ed. 203/250), 36 x 36 inches. Clara S. Peck Fund purchase. 2000.22.11. © 2001 Andy Warhol Foundation for the Visual Arts/ARS, New York

Notes

1. Lydia L. Wyckoff, ed. *Visions and Voices: Native American Paintings from the Philbrook Museum of Art* (Tulsa: Philbrook Museum of Art, 1996), 142.

stories his father told. "He knew all of Geronimo's medicine songs. I can remember old people with tears running down their cheeks when he sang about things they remembered." When he taught at the Institute of American Indian Arts in Santa Fe in the 1970s, Hauser/Haozous told his students to "be an Indian but allow for something creative too."

New generations of Native American artists have done just that, creating art dealing with issues of identity as in Jaune Quick-to-See Smith's *NDN (for life)* (Plate 87) and works that redress history as Diego Romero does in his ceramic, *Never Forget: Jim Thorpe, All American* (Plate 56). Cherokee artist Kay WalkingStick (*Tucson Series VI*, Plate 88) and Yurok artist Rick Bartow (*Dog, Deer, and Me*, Plate 50) redefine their relationships to nature and to the land. Native American artists and Indians everywhere are reclaiming their lives in a West that is America.

and Cowboys!

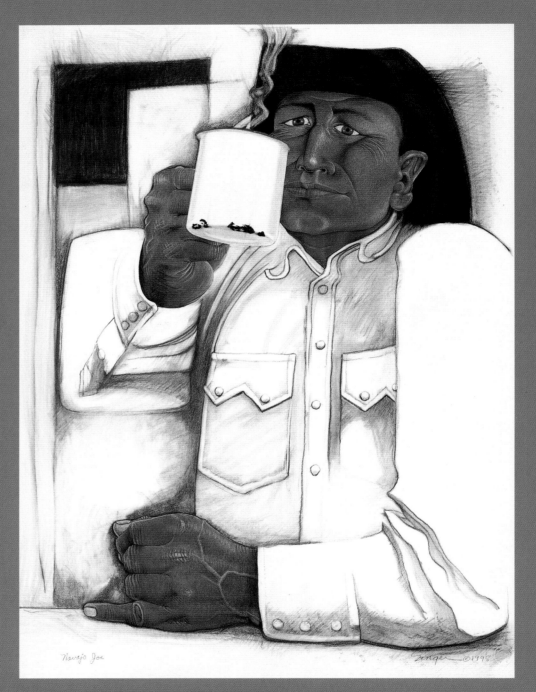

59. Ed Singer, *Navajo Joe*, 1998. Mixed media on paper, 28½ x 22 inches. Clara S. Peck Fund purchase. 2000.9.1

and Cowboys!

O you youths, Western youths,
So impatient, full of action, full of manly pride and friendship,
Plain I see you Western youths. . . .

—Walt Whitman, "Pioneers! O Pioneers!" in *Leaves of Grass*

The cowboy is a distinct genus. He is unlike any other being . . .

—*Leslie's Illustrated Weekly*, 1881

THE ROMANTIC COWBOY of the American frontier was not always the popular hero portrayed in western history and legend. It took the influence of the charismatic scout and showman Buffalo Bill Cody to transform the image of the cowboy from that of "armed desperado" to the rough-riding but chivalrous symbol of the Wild West.

The American cowboy most likely was born a Spanish vaquero herding cattle in the Southwest; he became familiar in the 1800s as the rough character riding with cattle on the western grazing grounds once occupied by buffalo. When Buffalo Bill's Wild West show began touring in the early 1880s, Cody's cowboys were champions of the plains, rescuing helpless easterners from bandits, riding for the Pony Express, defending covered wagon trains from attacking Indians—engaging in just about everything except tending cattle on the open range, unless it was chasing and "stringing up" rustlers. Cowboys rode bucking broncos, raced mustangs, were cowgirls. Trick riders and sure-shots like Annie Oakley (*Annie Oakley*, Plate 64) also rode those broncs and performed magic with lassos and guns.

Artists did their part to popularize cowboys, largely by illustrating western magazines and books that were popular around the turn of the twentieth century. Without question, the two greatest cowboy artists

60. Edward James Fraughton, *The Spirit of Wyoming*, 1978. Bronze (ed. 6/30), 42⅜ x 39¼ x 30⅜ inches. Museum purchase. 84.40

were Frederic Remington and Charles M. Russell, the "primary visual mythmakers of the Old West."[1] Remington was born in New York but grew up reading accounts of the western adventures of explorers such as George Catlin and Lewis and Clark. After his father's death, he left Yale to travel in the West. Fascinated by the cowboy life he witnessed and convinced that "the wild riders and the vacant land were about to vanish forever," he decided to become an artist to document the passing scene at a time when he believed that, "most people didn't know whether cowboys milked dairy cows or fought in the Revolution."[2] Remington's cowboys were meant to represent universal types rather than individuals (*Arizona Cowboy*, Plate 67); collectively, they were the West.

Always attracted to the heroic, Remington was drawn to the Indian Wars, which were approaching their end when he went West (*The Winter Campaign*, Plate 68). As an artist war correspondent, he published hundreds of views of the Indian Wars in American magazines. His illustrations of the Geronimo campaign in the Southwest appeared frequently in *Harper's Weekly*.

New Jersey artist Charles Schreyvogel also produced paintings that glorified the "Indian-fighting army." Never an illustrator, he traveled west every year to sketch, collect artifacts, and talk to war veterans about their experiences, then returned to his Hoboken studio to complete his paintings. In 1900, after photographs of Schreyvogel's prize-winning painting, *My Bunkie*, appeared in New York newspapers, a critic wrote, "If you should ask any American soldier who are his favorite painters, he would answer quick as a flash: Charles Schreyvogel and Frederic Remington."[3]

By the end of 1900, Remington was disillusioned with the West. From Santa Fe he wrote to his wife at their home in New Rochelle, New York, that he would "never come West again—it is all brick buildings—

derby hats and blue overhauls—it spoils my early illusions—and they are my capital."[4] In 1904 he wrote, "The West is no longer the West of picturesque and stirring events. . . . The Cowboy—the real thing, mark you, not the tame hired hand—disappeared with the advent of the wire fence."[5]

Charles Marion Russell, nicknamed the Cowboy Genius, was "driven by a consuming fascination with human nature."[6] This and Russell's ability to intuitively capture the decisive moment in the scenes he painted were his real gifts; as a self-taught artist, his technique was secondary. A true westerner, Russell was born near Saint Louis in 1864, when it was still in the West, and traveled to Montana in 1880 to work on a sheep ranch, the first of several jobs that immersed him in cowboy and Indian life. He worked for eleven years as a night wrangler, which left him free during the day to explore the countryside and make art. He completed his first major oil in 1885. *Breaking Camp* depicts several cowboys on bucking broncos in a wild tangle like the ones in *One Down, Two to Go* (Plate 70) and *A Mix Up* (Plate 71).

Russell also was a sculptor. The story goes that the first artwork he made in Montana was a small wax sculpture of a horse. For years, he made wax and clay models that he used as studies, but until he first cast a work in bronze in 1904, he hadn't taken his models seriously. "What he had created . . . were generally small figures crafted from a lump of wax he carried in his pocket. Once completed, these were either given to friends or mashed into a ball for him to reuse."[7]

Cowboy art did not die with Remington and Russell, but it has changed over time, just as the notion of cowboys has changed. Today's cowboy is not created so much by occupation (tending cattle) as by attitude (identifying with the "cowboy West"). Many cowboys today have never been near a horse or cow, let alone a working ranch. Working cowboys and rodeo riders tend to be

61. Frederic Remington, *The Bronco Buster*, modeled in 1895. Bronze (ed. cast 252), 22 7/16 x 21 3/8 x 13 7/8 inches. Gift of the Rockwell Foundation. 85.57

62. Charles Schreyvogel, *The Last Drop*, modeled
c. 1900, cast 1903. Bronze (23), 12 x 18 x 5
inches. Gift of the Rockwell Foundation. 83.30

63. Charles Schreyvogel, *An Unexpected Enemy*,
1900. Oil on canvas, 33¾ x 24¾ inches. Gift of
the Rockwell Foundation. 78.67

SHE WAS NOT ONLY the greatest rifle shot for a woman that ever lived, but I doubt if her character could be matched anywhere outside of a saint. . . . I had heard cowboys who traveled with the [Buffalo] Bill [Wild West] Show speak of her almost in reverence. They loved her. She was a marvelous woman, kindest hearted, most thoughtful, a wonderful Christian woman.

—*Will Rogers*

64. Andy Warhol, *Annie Oakley*, 1986. Silkscreen on paper (ed. 203/250), 36 x 36 inches. Clara S. Peck Fund purchase. 2000.22.8. © 2001 Andy Warhol Foundation for the Visual Arts/ARS, New York

65. John Edward Borein, *The Passing Herd* or *Cattle and Horsemen*, c. 1930s. Watercolor on multi-ply board, 10⅜ x 15⅜ inches. Clara S. Peck bequest. 83.46.10

women almost as often as they are men. Contemporary artist Ed Singer's subtly humorous, mixed-media portrait, *Navajo Joe* (Plate 59) reminds us that Indians sometimes are cowboys, too.

For centuries, artists in the West have devoted themselves to portraying the buffalo, the horse, the Indian, the cowboy—all epic figures in the fascinating, ever-changing tableaux of western experience, and the landscapes that have shaped them. These images of the American West have become the art of America. Where is the American West? It surely can be found in the art that celebrates it.

66. Frank Tenney Johnson, *The Morning Shower*, 1927. Oil on canvas, 36 x 28 inches. Gift of the Rockwell Foundation. 78.35

WITH THE BUFFALO went the Indian and with the cattle came the cowboy. Created by that northward sweep of the long-horned herds he was briefly the dominant figure in the whole Southwest. . . . The period of his importance was hardly more than a generation. It came to an end when money and fences laid hold of the grasslands. But he survives in the imagination of men. . . . He is an immortal stereotype.

—Harvey Ferguson, *Rio Grande*, 1933

67. Frederic Remington, *The Arizona Cowboy*, 1901. Pastel and graphite on paper, 30 x 24 inches. Gift of the Rockwell Foundation. 78.45

68. Frederic Remington, *The Winter Campaign*, 1909. Oil on canvas, 27 x 40⅛ inches. Clara S. Peck Fund purchase. 87.11

69. Frederic Remington, *Cutting Out a Steer*, April 1888. Oil on academy board, 18 x 18 inches. Gift of the Rockwell Foundation. 78.46

70. Charles Marion Russell, *One Down, Two to Go*, 1902. Watercolor on paper, 19⅝ x 29½ inches. Gift of the Rockwell Foundation. 78.55

71. Charles Marion Russell, *A Mix Up*, 1910. Oil on canvas, 30 x 48 inches. Gift of Robert F. Rockwell, Jr. 78.54

Notes

1. William H. Goetzmann and William N. Goetzmann, *The West of the Imagination* (New York: W. W. Norton & Company, 1986), 237.

2. Wayne Craven, *Sculpture in America* (University of Delaware, 1968), 532.

3. *West of the Imagination*, 212.

4. Robert R. White, *Territorial Artists of New Mexico, 1846–1912* (unpublished Ph.D. dissertation, University of New Mexico, 1993), 133.

5. *Sculpture in America, 535.*

6. Peter Hassrick, *Charles M. Russell* (New York: Harry N. Abrams, Inc., Publishers, in association with The National Museum of American Art, Smithsonian Institution, 1989), 7.

7. *Charles M. Russell,* 85.

The Southwest

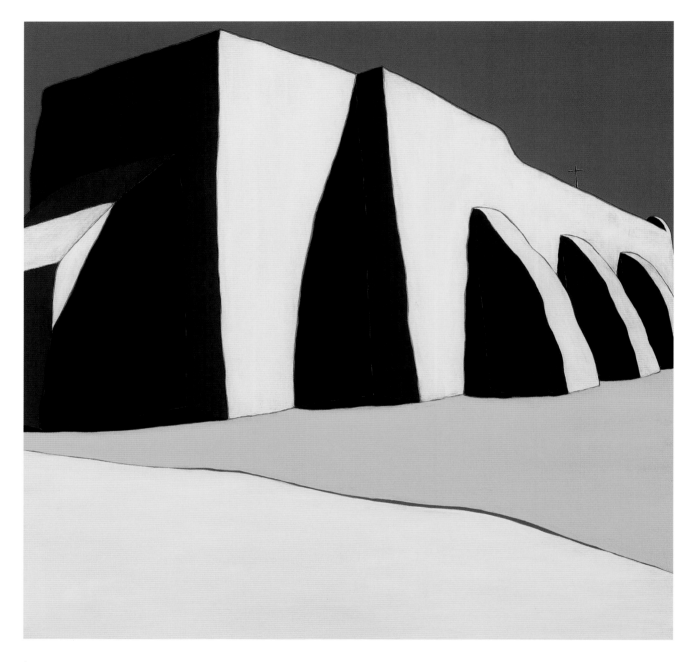

72. Harold Joe Waldrum, *La Iglesia de San Ildefonso*, 1985. Acrylic on canvas, 54 x 54 inches. Gift of Joanna Wurtele. 87.31

The Southwest

The moment I saw the brilliant, proud morning shine high up over the deserts. . . something stood still in my soul, and I started to attend. . . . What splendour! Only the tawny eagle could really sail out into the splendour of it all.

—D. H. Lawrence, *New Mexico*, 1928

Any man who is really an artist will find the Southwest . . . a region where the ingenuity, the imagination, and love of God are . . . visible at every turn. . . . It is high time for the artists to come upon the Southwest.

—Charles F. Lummis, "The Artist's Paradise," in *Out West*, 1908

SOON AFTER GENERAL STEPHEN WATTS KEARNY led his Army of the West into New Mexico, in 1846, claiming it for the United States, artists began to arrive in the Southwest to explore and document this new yet ancient land. They arrived as soldiers, expedition artists, and adventurers.

John Mix Stanley went there with Kearny, becoming the first artist to illustrate the Southwest for easterners. Worthington Whittredge went to the Southwest with a military expedition in 1866; Peter Moran followed the railroad to New Mexico in 1880. Between 1886 and 1907, Frederic Remington made many sketching trips through New Mexico territory (which included present-day Arizona). Scores of artists traveled there to paint landscapes, Native Americans, and Hispanics for the Santa Fe Railway well into the twentieth century.

But it wasn't until Cincinnati artist Joseph Henry Sharp visited Taos, New Mexico, in the 1890s and told young artists Ernest L. Blumenschein and Bert Phillips about its stunning landscapes and exotic natives that the Southwest became a destination instead of just another stop on artists' tours. The story of the broken wagon wheel that landed Blumenschein and Phillips in Taos in September 1898 has become

ERNEST L. BLUMENSCHEIN was a founder, in 1898, of the Taos art colony and helped establish the Taos Society of Artists (TSA), which existed from 1915 to 1927. An outstanding academy-trained painter, Blumenschein's style shifted gradually toward modernist principles and techniques. By 1936, when he painted *Jury for Trial of a Sheepherder for Murder*, which he considered his "finest and most successful" painting, he had been exposed to the social realist painting produced by Mexican and American artists during the Depression. The painting reflects Blumenschein's compassion for Hispanics of the Taos Valley who were caught between their traditions and customs and twentieth-century American jurisprudence. Although Blumenschein's daughter, Helen Blumenschein, recalled in 1979 (*Recuerdos: Early Days of the Blumenschein Family*) that the bespectacled figure peering from behind the jury box was a "blind Taos Indian, symbolizing Blind Justice," it now is generally believed that Blumenschein painted his self-portrait as a witness to the proceedings.

The painting portrays a Taos jury made up of Hispanics, probably Penitentes, members of a religious brotherhood native to northern New Mexico. According to Laura M. Bickerstaff, a friend and early biographer of TSA members, "The title is self explanatory– twelve of a rough sheepherder's peers sitting in the jury box. Blumenschein says that he used only one model for all the jurymen, but he would go uptown and look at the sheepherders lounging around the plaza, then do the heads from memory. He did not do 'Jury' until a year after the actual trial, but he kept thinking of it and finally had to paint it." (Laura M. Bickerstaff, *Pioneer Artists of Taos*.)

A Penitente sheepherder had killed a hiker who startled him as he neared the sheep camp. The Anglo hiker and his companions had violated the well-known procedure for approaching isolated camps, and the sheepherder's peers knew that he had acted reasonably under the circumstances. Nevertheless, they were required to judge him according to the alien laws of the United States, symbolized by the featureless portrait of George Washington over the alcove where they were assembled.

—S.C.

73. Ernest Blumenschein, *Jury for Trial of a Sheepherder for Murder*, 1936. Oil on canvas, 46 x 30 inches. Clara S. Peck Fund purchase. 97.13

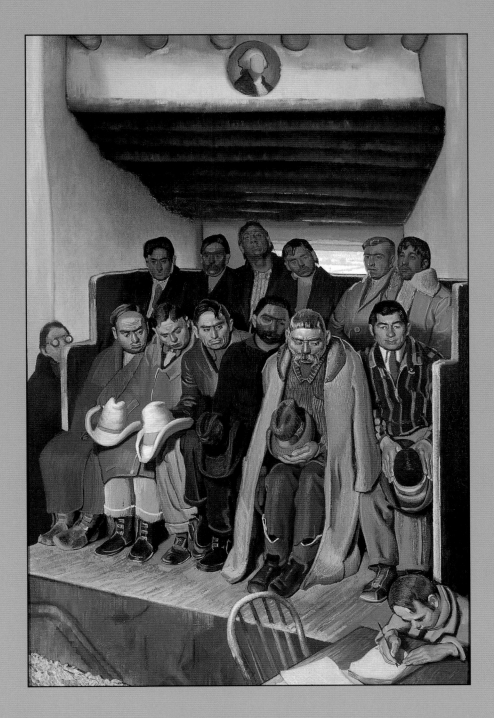

74. E. Martin Hennings, *The Teacher*, c. 1925. Oil on canvas, 15½ x 19¼ inches. Gift of Sandra Rockwell Herron. 78.962

New Mexico has almost made a landscape painter out of me, although I believe my strongest work is in figures. . . . In figure subjects I think I find my greatest inspiration.

—E. Martin Hennings, in Bickerstaff, *Pioneer Artists of Taos*

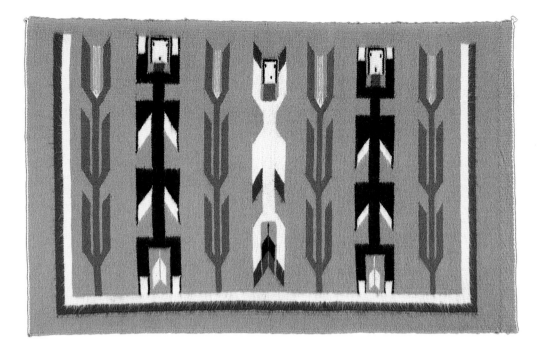

75. Artist Unknown (Navajo), Textile, c. 1965–1970. Commercial and handspun wool yarns, natural colors and aniline dye, 22½ x 33¾ inches. Gift of Sandra Rockwell Herron. 99.31.57

myth. Upon seeing the remote village for themselves, they decided to end their summer's painting expedition and remain in Taos to establish an art colony.

The words enchanted, magical, and spiritual frequently are used to describe the Southwest. It *is* truly different from other regions of the West. There is a pervasive aura there that D.H. Lawrence brilliantly termed "spirit of place." The stunning, sometimes surreal features of the landscape, and Native Americans' and Hispanics' colorful religious rituals, offered a wellspring of subjects for artist's brush and writer's pen. New Mexico author Frank Waters insisted that "the vast sage desert undulates with almost imperceptible tides like the oceans." Other writers regarded the land as alive: "It has a tensile strength . . . a thrusting power," wrote one. Lawrence summed up his fascination with the Southwest when he declared, "It was always beauty, *always!*"[1]

The Southwest has long been rich in Native artists who create fine

76. Artist Unknown (Santo Domingo), polychrome ceramic dough bowl, before 1909. Ceramic, 6 ¼ inches x 14 inches diameter. Gift of Robert F. Rockwell III. 93.12.6

textiles, jewelry, ceramics, wood carvings, and paintings, to say nothing of the sculptural vernacular architecture of the pueblos and mission churches. Georgia O'Keeffe once confessed that she "had to paint" the Ranchos de Taos church. Like O'Keeffe, who often painted "fragments of things" that she felt made her statement "as well as or better than the whole could,"[2] contemporary artist Harold Waldrum finds inspiration in the architectural details of northern New Mexico's Hispanic and Indian Mission churches, as in *La Iglesia de San Ildefonso* (Plate 72). Carlos Vierra, the first painter to live in Santa Fe, was devoted to the local Hispanic architecture, seen in his lyrical *New Mexico Afternoon* (Plate 83); his paintings of Pueblo mission churches inspired the creation of the popular "Santa Fe style" of architecture.

To the delight of early artists in the Southwest, this painters' paradise was located fortuitously in the United States—it was *American!* Beginning in the late 1800s, artists were urged, even admonished, to turn from European subjects to paint America, "as Americans." Thomas Moran declared that the very future of American art depended on artists "being true to our own country." The flamboyant explorer-journalist Charles Lummis coined the phrase, "See America First!"[3] With evidence of ancient cultures abounding, no region of the country could claim to be more "American" than the Southwest.

By 1915, artists who gathered in Taos every summer to paint, and

77. Eanger Irving Couse, *The Apprentice*, 1910. Oil on canvas, 35 x 45¾ inches. Gift of Robert F. Rockwell, Jr. 75.1

a few who had settled there, founded the Taos Society of Artists to promote their work in art centers in the East and Midwest. Their paintings of Indians and Hispanics engaged in everyday activities or religious ceremonies, such as Walter Ufer's *Along the Rio Grande* (Plate 2) and Sharp's *Gift Dance Drummers* (Plate 82), were popular and critically successful wherever they were exhibited. Taos and Santa Fe became mandatory stops on artists' western tours and the final destination for many more.

Rather than violent battles or frenetic hunting scenes, Taos Society and other artists mostly painted Indians and Hispanics performing domestic tasks or creating art, and often reproduced their weavings, pottery, baskets, jewelry, religious art, and architecture in their own paintings, either as straightforward still lifes or in narrative scenes as

78. Eanger Irving Couse, *The Cliff Dwellers,*
1911. Oil on canvas, 45¾ x 35 inches. Gift of
Robert F. Rockwell, Jr. 78.25

They wear squash-flowers cut in silver
And carve the sun on canyon walls;
Their words are born of storm and
calyx,
Eagles, and waterfalls.

They weave the thunder in the basket,
And paint the lightning in the bowl;
Taking the village to the rainbow,
And the rainbow to the soul.

—Haniel Long, *Indians*

79. Eanger Irving Couse, *Ben Luhan, left; John Concha, right; in the artist's studio*, 1903; from *Ten Photographs: A Limited Edition Portfolio*, 1998. Selenium toned silver print, 7´ x 9´ inches. Clara S. Peck Fund purchase. 2000.10.6

80. Eanger Irving Couse, *Jerry Mirabel examining a decorated garment*, 1911; from *Ten Photographs by Eanger Irving Couse, N.A. (1866–1936): A Limited Edition Portfolio*, 1998. Selenium toned silver print, 9½ x 7½ inches. Clara S. Peck Fund purchase. 2000.10.2

81. Gene Kloss, *Song of Creation*, 1949. Drypoint on paper, 12 x 15 inches. Clara S. Peck Fund purchase. 97.20

models' costumes, furnishings, and backdrops. Ernest Blumenschein spoke for many when he wrote about the importance to immigrant artists of Native American art (textile, Plate 75; polychrome ceramic dough bowl, Plate 76). "Their contribution to art has been invaluable," he declared. We come out here to learn from them and find an apparently inexhaustible store of beauty and originality."[4]

E. Martin Hennings created a quiet commentary on the conflict between tradition and the modern in *The Teacher* (Plate 74). In the painting, a man wearing traditional braids and wrapped in a blanket is absorbed by the drum beat, while his young student, dressed in blue jeans and shirt rather than traditional garb, watches respectfully if somewhat skeptically. Eanger Irving Couse painted an older artist teaching the traditional art of pottery design to a young boy in *The Apprentice* (Plate 77), yet no hint of disruptive modernity intrudes on the tranquil scene. Couse frequently returned to the theme of a father instructing his children, as in *The Cliff Dwellers* (Plate 78), especially when his Taos Indian model began to raise a family.[5]

After spending six years in the art colony, Russian-born artist Nicolai Fechin left Taos in 1933 to live in California, "the *end* of the *Far West*."[6] In California he left behind the bright, saturated palette he had preferred in Taos to embrace the softer mood of the southern California coast, which he painted in the impressionist *Sorrento Valley* (Plate 85).

82. Joseph Henry Sharp, *The Gift Dance Drummers*, c. 1910–1920. Oil on canvas, 29½ x 39½ inches. Gift of the Rockwell Foundation. 78.61

84. Howard Cook, *Snow and 'Dobe,* 1926. Linocut on paper, 11¾ x 9¼ inches. Clara S. Peck Fund purchase. 99.23.4

83. Carlos Vierra, *New Mexico Afternoon,* c. 1920. Oil on board, 15¾ x 19⅞ inches. Clara S. Peck Fund purchase. 2000.8

Through the decades the Southwest has become an ever more popular mecca for artists of all kinds, and a major market for both Native and non-Native art. While traditional arts are still practiced, contemporary artists seek new inspiration in the landscape and cultures that inspired the first artists of the Southwest. Cochiti artist Diego Romero blends traditional shapes with contemporary imagery in his pottery, whose surfaces he treats as "canvas" for his artistic and political statements. Wilson Hurley steps outside his back door in the foothills just east of Albuquerque to paint ethereal landscapes of the Sandia

85. Nicolai Fechin, *Sorrento Valley*, 1925. Oil on canvas, 30⅛ x 36¼ inches. Acquired with the assistance of Joanna Wurtele. 90.14

Mountains (*La Cueva Cañon, Sandias,* Plate 18).

As early as 1904, N.C. Wyeth described the sensation that artists continue to experience in the Southwest when he observed, "The life is wonderful, strange—the fascination of it clutches me like some unseen animal—it seems to whisper, 'Come back, you belong here, this is your real home.'"[7]

86. William Herbert "Buck" Dunton, *Deer Hunters' Camp*, 1926. Oil on canvas, 20 x 16 inches. Gift of Mrs. George J. Openhym. 78.28

Notes

1. Arnold Skolnick, ed., *Paintings of the Southwest*, with an introduction by Suzan Campbell (New York: Clarkson Potter, 1994), 6.

2. Georgia O'Keeffe, *Georgia O'Keeffe* (New York: The Viking Press, 1976), no page.

3. Sandra D'Emilio and Suzan Campbell, V*isions & Visionaries: The Art and Artists of the Santa Fe Railway* (Salt Lake City: Peregrine Smith Books, 1991), 2.

4. Ernest L. Blumenschein, "Appreciation of Indian Art," *El Palacio* 6 [24 May 1919], 179.

5. Virginia Couse Leavitt, *Eanger Irving Couse: Image Maker for America* (Albuquerque, NM: The Albuquerque Museum, 1991), 151.

6. William H. Goetzmann and William N. Goetzmann, *The West of the Imagination* (New York: W. W. Norton & Company, 1986), 71.

7. N. C. Wyeth, in *Paintings of the Southwest*, 128.

The Indian as Artist

led between

worlds navigating

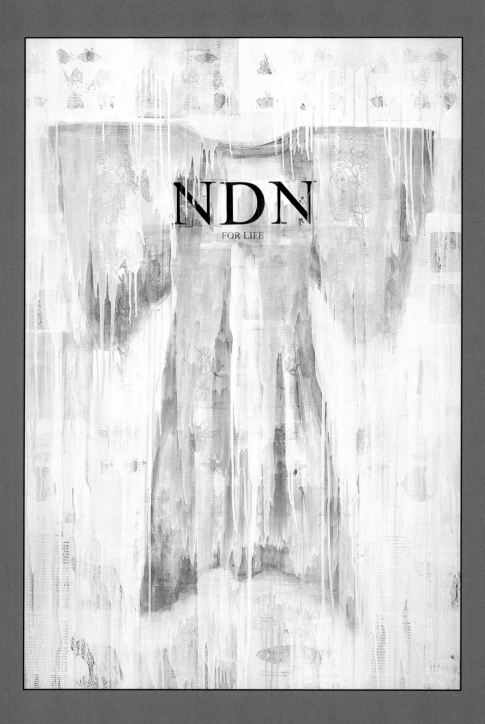

87. Jaune Quick-To-See Smith, *NDN (for life)*,
2000. Mixed media on canvas, 72 x 48 inches.
Gift of Joanna Wurtele. 2000.13

By KATHLEEN E. ASH-MILBY

The Indian as Artist
Native American Art at the Rockwell Museum of Western Art

IN 1999, CHEROKEE ARTIST SARA BATES quietly entered the Rockwell Museum of Western Art (RMWA) to install one of her "Honoring Circles." In complete privacy, she said her prayers of honor to the Old Ones, the members of her clan, the Wolf Clan, "and all that has gone before."[1] She then knelt on the floor of the gallery and slowly built an equal-armed cross within a circle using materials gathered from the earth, including stones, feathers, seashells and sand. The finished piece, titled *Honoring Mother Earth* (Fig. 3), was both a tribute to creative forces of the earth and evocative testimony to the continuum of Native American culture and art. "We've been making this sign for a very long time. . . . We've made it on rocks. We've made it in baskets or beadwork. I make it . . . with these things. And each generation makes it differently."[2] The installation created a stir in the community, and was deemed a "must-see" exhibition by the local paper.[3] Bates's work was both a visible and fitting milestone on the museum's journey into new territory in "western" art, the world of contemporary Native American art.

The RMWA began to consider collecting contemporary Native American art as recently as 1998, when the newly appointed director, Stuart Chase,[4] began conversations with Kay WalkingStick, a renowned

Fig. 3. *Honoring Mother Earth: An Installation by Sara Bates.* Mixed media installation, 12-foot diameter, Rockwell Museum of Western Art, Corning, New York, March 26–May 9, 1999. Rockwell Museum of Western Art Archives.

88. Kay WalkingStick, *Tucson Series VI*, 1990. Mixed dry media on stretched paper on a ground of sculptmetal, 22¾ x 44¾ inches. Clara S. Peck Fund purchase. 99.24.2

Cherokee artist, Ithaca resident, and professor of art at Cornell University. WalkingStick has long been a proponent for the recognition of Native American art in the wider art world. As one of the few self-identified Native American artists to break the race barrier, exemplified by her inclusion in the modern art collection of the Metropolitan Museum of Art, she acknowledges that "Indian artists are still ghet-toized."[5] What better place to feature Native artists than in a western art museum, a place where Native people have long been a part of the landscape and have been only recently recognized as having voices themselves?

Chase developed an interest in this area of the art world as early as 1981 when he assisted with the installation of "Confluences of Tradition and Change," a traveling exhibition of contemporary and historic

Native American art at the Museum of the Southwest in Midland, Texas. In subsequent years, his interest continued to brew as he became a regular on the Santa Fe gallery circuit, meeting artists, curators, and dealers. Chase was also impressed by the steps taken by other museums of western art, including the Eiteljorg Museum of American Indians and Western Art in Indianapolis, Indiana, and the National Cowboy and Western Heritage Museum in Oklahoma City, Oklahoma.[6]

To prepare the RMWA for the new direction he wanted to take the collection, in 1998 Chase invited WalkingStick to speak to the museum board. Using her art to communicate her message, WalkingStick brought along *Talking Leaves* (1993), a handmade book of self-portraits that explores her travels and travails as a Native American artist. She emphasized the importance of Native American artists' "right to identify themselves [as Indian], rather than being identified by others."[7]

In years past, most displays of western art primarily featured images of Native Americans through the eyes of white, male artists. These interpretations consisted largely of romanticized images of Native people captured on canvas, paper, and in bronze. Work by Native artists was often limited to historic "ethnographic" material consisting of artifacts, trophies, and trinkets. Beautifully made, though often humble, these objects did not challenge the viewer, but instead reinforced notions of "true" Indians living in a timeless past untouched by the modern world. The RMWA's own collection of historic Native American art reflects this old approach, consisting primarily of work created by the hands of anonymous bead workers, ceramicists, basket makers, and weavers (see Plates 75, 76, and 89).

But when is an Indian an artist? Is it true, as the cliché goes, that Indians have no word for art, therefore everything they do is art? Or do Native American artifacts belong in an art museum at all? Anthropological collections were traditionally created to serve as windows into the lives of Native peoples. Collecting Native American objects as art rather than as curiosities or items of scientific study is still

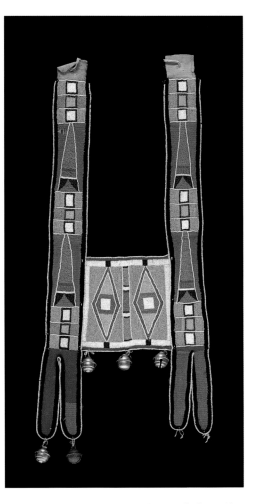

89. Artist Unknown (Crow), Beaded martingale, 1870–1890. Glass beads, leather, wool trade cloth, metal bells, 39½ x 15½ inches. Gift of Sandra Rockwell Herron. 91.69

Spontaneous Combustion

Sometimes when an Indian boy loves
a white girl and vice versa

it's like waking up
with half of the world

on fire. You don't know
if you should throw water

onto those predictable flames
or let the whole goddamn thing burn.

       –Sherman Alexie, *First Indian on the Moon*, 1993

90. Rosalie Favell, *Navigating by Our Grandmothers*, from *Plain(s) Warrior Artist*, 2000. Iris/Giclee print, 30 x 32½ inches. Clara S. Peck Fund purchase. 2000.24

91. Janice Ortiz, *Zozobra*, 1999. Ceramic, 12 x 7 x 5½ inches. Acquired with the assistance of Dwight Lanmon. 99.19.1

a less common approach; many great Indian art collections reside in natural history museums. Yet even though the RMWA was created as a western art museum, Native American objects were often collected to illustrate non-Indians' interpretation of the Indian presence in the West. They were used as props to complement a story told from the non-Indian's viewpoint. A significant portion of these objects might be grouped under the genre of tourist art, particularly many items in the Southwest collection (Plate 75).

Contemporary art by Native Americans resists this type of simple categorization. Some Native artists do continue using traditional techniques and forms, but others have embraced non-traditional materials and subjects from the so-called "white-man's world," and many more combine the two in exhilarating new ways. Like other art, Native American art has continued to grow and change, reflecting the new experiences and resources available to the artists. The category of contemporary Native American art is defined only by the maker's identity, not by technique, materials, or subject matter.

By 1999, the Museum was ready to make its first forays into this "new" world by hosting the installation by Bates and acquiring work by other artists which reflects the diversity of Native American art. Among the first acquisitions were two works on paper by Kay WalkingStick and *Zozobra* (Plate 91), a ceramic piece created in 1999 by Cochiti artist Janice Ortiz. WalkingStick's *Tucson Series VI* (Plate 88) and *Tucson Series VIII*, both created in 1990, are two small, mixed dry-media works on stretched paper, and are related to larger diptychs she later created and for which she is well known. WalkingStick's work is highly abstract and personal, exploring the relationship between the memory of the land and eternity.

The masterful use of design and abstraction is indicative of both historic and contemporary Native American art. Historic examples in the museum collection range from painted designs on historic pueblo ceramics (Plate 76) to rich patterns in basketry and beadwork (Plate 89).

Ho-chunk artist Truman Lowe deconstructs and rebuilds through abstraction in his two interpretations of a feather basket (Plates 1 and 29). In his bronze, the artist has focused on the very edge of a basket, a mere slice of the whole. While the bronze appears to be light as a feather, the wood sculpture is an exploration of the basket's solidity, form and saturated color. By focusing on a fragmented view of the interior of a Comanche lodge, or tipi, photographer Walter Bigbee's bold composition, *Numu Kahni Wahtanuu* (Plate 94), also manages to capture an ethereal experience: Prayers said over burning sage or cedar are believed to be carried to the creator on the drifting smoke.

Ortiz's *Zozobra* represents the work of artists who still use traditional mediums and forms, but with a contemporary twist. The figure is a playful depiction of an effigy burned at Santa Fe's annual fiesta since the 1920s. Humorous and satirical renderings of outsiders to pueblo society have a long tradition in Cochiti ceramics, documented as early as the 1890s.[8] Other contemporary ceramic artists represented in the collection include Diego Romero, also Cochiti, known for his narrative painting style reminiscent of ancient Mimbres pottery, and Christine Nofchissey McHorse, a Navajo highly influenced by pueblo traditions (Plate 26). Works in traditional mediums such as pottery, basketry and beadwork, have often been defined as "craft" for being made of "low art" materials. But where does the bronze rendition of a Klickatat basket (Plate 92) by Warm Springs/Wasco/Yakama artist Lillian Pitt fit? These artists further blur the line between traditional and contemporary, craft and art.

What contemporary Native artists do share is the common bond of

92. Lillian Pitt, *Klickitat Basket with Masks*, 2000, bronze, 14 x 12¾ x 13⅜ inches. Clara S. Peck Fund purchase. 2000.27

THE AMERICAN WEST

93. Judith Lowry, *Family: Love's Unbreakable Heaven*, 1995. Acrylic on canvas. 67⅞ x 85 inches overall (61⅛ x 29, 51 x 50, 67⅞ x 55 inches). Clara S. Peck Fund purchase. 2000.40.1–3

THIS IMAGE REFERS to a Christmas day in the early 1950s, when my family and I were living in Germany. My parents had managed to make a Plains style Indian costume for my little brother to play in. They did not make one for me, however. I did not feel deprived as my folks were always generous with us at Christmas time. What was significant for me, at that moment, was watching my brother dance around in front of our home movie camera and realizing for the first time that he was an Indian. I knew that I was part Indian too because my dad had told me many times. But what was happening here was the realization that my brother's looks identified him as such. I take after my mother who was Australian of European descent. My brother took after my father, obviously native in appearance. For the first time, I understood that I came from a racially mixed family.

—Judith Lowry, artist's statement, 1999

Native identity. As Jaune Quick-to-See Smith states so poignantly in her painting, *NDN (for life)* (Plate 87), many Native people live with their Indian identity as if it were emblazoned on their shirts. But the meaning of being a Native person is never quite so superficial. Like the translucent surface of her painting, multiple meanings and complexities are layered beneath, sometimes only partially visible on the surface.

Like their predecessors, Native artists must navigate the shifting realities of contemporary life. In contrast to the picturesque visions of Indian life in traditional western art, being Indian today means dealing with many demons, from substance abuse and poverty to cultural bigotry. These issues are tackled head-on by many artists. For instance, Diego Romero addresses social problems, which continue to subtly erode Indian communities. *Never Forget: Jim Thorpe, All American* (Plate 56), pays tribute to nationally-revered athlete Jim Thorpe (1888–1952). Though Thorpe, a Potawatomi, is a culture hero to Native people, until recent years the disposition of his remains seemed forgotten. Some time after his death they were removed to the town, Jim Thorpe, Pensylvania. The trophy, or urn-shaped, vase draws attention to both his accomplishments as an athlete and, in death, his physical removal from his tribe and homeland.

As intermarriage between Indian people and non-Indians increases, more and more artists are addressing the complex issues surrounding mixed-blood identity. In *Navigating by Our Grandmothers* (Plate 90), by Rosalie Favell, the artist and her sister sit astride a horse against a constellation featuring two of her cultural guides: her European and Cree Métis grandmothers. In her triptych, *Family: Love's Unbreakable Heaven* (Plate 93), Judith Lowry, of Mountain Maidu, Hamowi Pit River and Euro-Australian descent, captures the moment of clarity she experienced when she realized that she would be treated differently in her life because she looked less Indian than her brother. Sometimes being an Indian is about dealing with difficult identity issues such as these, and other times, as in one of Ed Singer's views of contemporary Navajo

94. Walter BigBee, *Nʉmʉ Kahni Wah-tanʉʉ*, 1994. Silver gelatin print (ed. 1/1/3), 13 x 10 inches. Clara S. Peck Fund purchase. 2000.18

Notes

1. Sara Bates, "Honoring." In *Native American Art in the Twentieth Century: Makers, Meanings, Histories*, W. Jackson Rushing, III, ed. (London and New York: Routledge, 1999), 199.

2. Sara Bates to Jeremy Ehrenreich, "Must-see exhibit draws similarities among all people, ages," *The Leader* (March 28, 1999), 1D.

3. Jeremy Ehrenreich, "Must-see exhibit draws similarities among all people, ages," *The Leader* (March 28, 1999), 1D-2D.

4. Stuart Chase became director of the Rockwell Museum of Western Art in 1997.

5. Charlene Touchette, "Interview: Kay WalkingStick," *THE* magazine, 3:2 (August 2000), 63.

6. The Eiteljorg Museum of American Indians and Western Art started awarding the Fellowship for Native American Fine Art in 1999; the National Cowboy and Western Heritage Museum contains the prestigious Arthur and Shifra Silberman Collection, an archive and collection of contemporary Native American art acquired in 1997.

7. Kay WalkingStick, personal communication, 2000.

8. Jonathan Batkin, Patricia Fogelman Lange, with the assistance of Robert V. Gallegos and Cheri Falkenstein-Doyle, "Human Figurines of Cochiti and Tesuque Pueblos, 1879–1920: Inspirations, Markets, and Consumers," *Clay People: Pueblo Indian Figurative Traditions*, Jonathan Batkin, ed. (Santa Fe: Wheelwright Museum of the American Indian), 42.

life, *Navajo Joe* (Plate 59), it is about finding the simple humor in a Navajo enjoying a cup of coffee.

In the coming years, the Museum plans to continue to build its Native American art collection by acquiring the work of well-established and recognized artists as well as supporting young and emerging artists, through educational programs, temporary exhibitions, and acquisitions. The sea change in attitudes may not have been obvious the day Sara Bates walked into the Museum, but the vision of the Native American as solely a subject of western art is continuing to change. Indians are no longer confined to subject status alone but are now recognized artists as well. By opening the doors of the Rockwell Museum of Western Art to Native American art, the Museum strives to give its audience a greater insight into the many cultures, complexities, and meanings of the western experience. And this time, the *Indian* is the artist.

Lastly, we return thanks to the Great Spirit, in whom is embodied all goodness, and who directs all things for the good of his children.

—Maurice Kenny, *Trail of the Wind*, in *The Remembered Earth*

Artists in the Collection

Born in Topeka, Kansas, **KENNETH MILLER ADAMS** (1897–1966) was youngest member of famed Taos Society of Artists. Studied at Art Institute of Chicago, 1916–17; in 1921, traveled to Paris, was influenced by Cezanne's art. On return, studied at New York Art Students League and its summer school in Woodstock, New York, with modernist painter Andrew Dasburg. Went to Santa Fe, 1924, then became permanent resident of Taos. Painted murals at University of New Mexico while artist in residence; remained to teach, 1942–63. Elected to National Academy of Design, 1961.

NORMAN AKERS (b. 1958), Osage and Pawnee, was born in Fairfax, Oklahoma. Earned B.F.A. from Kansas City Art Institute, 1982; received Certificate of Museum Training from Institute of American Indian Arts, Santa Fe, 1983. Awarded M.F.A. from University of Illinois, Champaign-Urbana, 1991. Large-scale paintings in oil explore personal and cultural symbols, memories, traditional beliefs. Professor of art, Institute of American Indian Arts, Santa Fe, New Mexico.

Born in small farming community of Rudyard, Montana, thirty miles south of Canadian border, landscape painter **CLYDE ASPEVIG** (b. 1951) began studying art at age nine; when only twelve, began oil painting under guidance of artist uncle. Graduated from Eastern Montana College, Billings, 1976, with degree in art education. Full-time painter since 1977, interested in sublime in nature. Lives in Clyde Park, Montana.

Haitian **JOHN JAMES AUDUBON** (1785–1851), born in Les Cayes of Creole and French parents, devoted career to painting birds and animals of North America. Before arriving in United States, in 1806, studied in France. Worked briefly as portrait painter, then compiled paintings for *The Birds of North America,* published in four volumes from 1827–38. Collected specimens in the field, took them to studio to create pastel and watercolor paintings from which volumes' hand-colored aquatints were made. Noted for dramatic presentation and scientific accuracy.

The younger son of John James Audubon, **JOHN WOODHOUSE AUDUBON** (1812–1862) was born in Henderson, Kentucky. Taught sketching by his father; in 1837 they explored bird life along Texas coast. After 1839, he lived in New York City, traveled in Europe and the West. Spent final years of life finishing father's book, *Quadrupeds of North America,* completing more than half of the illustrations.

RICK BARTOW (b. 1946), Yurok, was born in Newport, Oregon. Earned B. A. from Western Oregon State College. Awarded Eiteljorg Fellowship for Native American Fine Art, 2001. His pastel and graphite drawings, paintings, "assemblage" sculpture draw on Northwest Coast Native art, culture; self-portraits and figures in transformation appear throughout work. Resides with family in Oregon.

LEONARD BASKIN (1922–2000) was born in New Brunswick, New Jersey, studied sculpture at the Educational Alliance, New York City, 1937–43. In 1949, began making wood engravings, studied at Academie de la Grande Chaumiere, Paris, and Accademia di Belle Arti, Florence. Professor of sculpture at Smith College, Northhampton, Massachusetts.

Born in Germany, **GUSTAVE BAUMANN** (1881–1971) immigrated with family to Chicago. Returned to Germany, 1905, studied in Munich; was influenced by German Arts and Crafts movement. Back in United States, studied at Art Institute of Chicago, worked as commercial artist. In 1918, visited Taos, New Mexico. Stopped in Santa Fe on return to Chicago, was befriended by Museum of New Mexico associate director, who gave him studio in museum basement; he never left Santa Fe. Best known for etched, carved, colored, and printed woodblock prints, using up to seventeen blocks. Images ranged from intimate scenes to sweeping vistas such as Grand Canyon.

JOE NEIL BEELER (b. 1931) was born in Joplin, Missouri. Part Cherokee, spent childhood in northeastern Oklahoma, listened to grandfather tell stories of West. Studied at Tulsa (Oklahoma) University, Kansas State University, and Art Center School, Los Angeles. Decorated sets in Hollywood. Was youngest founding member of Cowboy Artists of America, 1964; served as president, 1982. Known for paintings, illustrations, sculpture. Interprets historical and contemporary cowboy and Indian subjects.

NATHAN BEGAYE (b. 1958), Navajo and Hopi, grew up near Tuba City, Arizona. Attended Institute of American Indian Art high school program, Santa Fe, New Mexico. Largely self-taught potter, influenced by Hopi ceramicist Otellie Loloma and exposure to international ceramic artists during summer program at Alfred (New York) University, 1986. Work combines traditional materials and techniques, modern interpretation. Lives in Santa Fe.

THOMAS DUNCAN BENRIMO (1887–1958) was San Francisco, California, native, son of English immigrants. After 1906 earthquake destroyed family home, moved to New York City, briefly attended Art Students League, became commercial artist, theatrical set designer. Taught at Pratt Institute, 1935–39. In 1939, moved to Taos to become easel painter. Among first New Mexico artists to paint in surrealist manner. After WWII,

painted mostly abstractions; also made prints and drawings.

GEORGE F. BENSELL (1837–1879) was born in Philadelphia, Pennsylvania; remained there his entire life. Showed talent as a youth, becoming portraitist before age twenty. Worked in oils and crayon. Exhibited at Pennsylvania Academy of Fine Arts, 1856–68. Known for historical and landscape painting, scenes featuring Indians are considered product of his imagination.

Born near Dusseldorf, Germany, **ALBERT BIERSTADT** (1830–1902) immigrated with family to New Bedford, Massachusetts, 1832. Studied in Dusseldorf, 1853–56; in 1857 traveled through Alps with American artists Worthington Whittredge and Sanford Robinson Gifford. Went West in 1859 in search of dramatic landscapes; soon became leader of "Rocky Mountain School" of artists. Interested in Romantic possibilities of mountain scenery, traveled to Yosemite Valley in 1863, painted it as place of almost supernatural wonder, rearranging and exaggerating outstanding features. In 1871, moved to California to be close to favorite scenery; in 1873, built San Francisco studio. By mid-1870s, was most popular western landscape painter in America; enjoyed international fame.

Comanche photographer **WALTER BIGBEE/ TUTSI WAI** (b. 1958) was born in Michigan. Studied at Rochester Institute of Technology, 1977–79. Worked in graphic art and commercial photography, including documentary and studio work in Washington and Virginia. Works primarily in black and white photography, emphasizing design and strong composition. Addresses environmental concerns, storytelling, the resurgence of the buffalo. Freelance photographer in Santa Fe. Manages family gallery and resides at Tesuque Pueblo, New Mexico.

EMIL BISTTRAM (1895–1976) immigrated with Hungarian family to New York's lower east side, studied at National Academy of Design, Cooper Union, and New York School of Fine and Applied Art. After opening commercial art business, decided to become fine artist. Taught at Parson's School of Design and Master Institute of United Artists, founded by Nicholas Roerich, Russian artist and mystic dedicated to "universal expression" in art. In 1931, after studying with Diego Rivera in Mexico while on Guggenheim Fellowship, went to Taos, opened town's first commercial art gallery and avant-garde Taos School of Art. In 1938, he helped form nationally recognized Transcendental Painting Group, to "carry painting beyond the appearance of the physical world." Died in Taos.

Born in Pittsburgh, Pennsylvania, **ERNEST LEONARD BLUMENSCHEIN** (1874–1960) grew up in Dayton, Ohio. Studied at Cincinnati Academy of Fine Arts, then at New York Art Students League. While attending Academie Julian in Paris, met American artist Joseph Henry Sharp who praised Taos as ideal place to paint. In 1897, went to Southwest on assignment for *McClure's Magazine*. In 1898 he and artist Bert Phillips traveled to Denver, bought wagon and team of horses, departed on painting trip. On 3 September 1898, broken wagon wheel sent him to nearby Taos to have it repaired. He and Phillips decided to remain, establish art colony; he departed after several months. After 1910, returned each spring to paint; in 1919 settled there. In 1915 was founding member of Taos Society of Artists. Resigned in 1923, helped form modernist New Mexico Painters group. Elected to National Academy of Design, 1927. In 1950s, poor health sent him south to Albuquerque; he painted cityscapes and Santa Fe Railway yards until his death.

Swiss "viewpainter" **KARL BODMER** (1809–1893) traveled to United States in 1832 with German Prince Maximilian to document North American Indians. Trained as engraver, he rendered precise, emotionally powerful images of Indians, animals, and landscape. Watercolors painted during journey up Missouri River are among best views of western frontier. Never returned to America. Paris exhibition of Native American pictures in 1836 was first in Europe.

A San Leandro, California, native, **JOHN EDWARD BOREIN** (1872–1945) moved with his family to Oakland, a center of California cattle industry. As a child, sketched cowboys, longhorn cattle, and horses. After just one month, left San Francisco Art Association Art School to work on ranches along California coast while sketching actively. In 1896, sent drawings of cowboy life to the magazine *The Land of Sunshine*, beginning career as illustrator. Around 1900, grew disillusioned with ranch life; established studio in parents' Oakland home. In 1907, moved to New York City. At Art Students League, mastered etching, remained devoted to medium, which provided steady income from print sales. Returning to California in 1919, produced hundreds of etchings and watercolors celebrating ranching life in southwestern United States and Mexico.

Self–taught Kiowa and Comanche painter **BLACKBEAR BOSIN** (1921–1980) was born near Anadarko, Oklahoma, but lived mostly in Wichita, Kansas. A frequent participant in Philbrook Art Center's Indian Annual painting competition, Tulsa, Oklahoma, his vivid, dramatic adaptation of traditional Indian painting reflected belief in artistic freedom in Native American art. Solo exhibition, Southern Plains Indian Museum and Craft Center, Indian Arts and Crafts Board, U.S. Department of Interior, Anadarko, Oklahoma, 1971.

DAVID BRADLEY (b. 1954), Chippewa and Sioux, was born in Eureka, California.

Attended Institute of American Indian Arts, Santa Fe, New Mexico, 1977–79; University of Arizona, 1979; College of Santa Fe, 1980. Best known for work in oil, acrylic, and printmaking, though he also works in ceramics and bronze. Satirical narrative paintings combine humor with commentary on political and cultural issues. Resides in Santa Fe.

Raised on family farm in Michigan's Upper Peninsula, **DUANE BRYERS** (b. 1911) spent high school years in northern Minnesota. After earning $3,000 from mural commission, went to New York City, worked as commercial artist. Moved to Tucson, Arizona, painted western scenes that made him famous. Won 1997 Prix de West Purchase and Buyers' Choice Award, Cowboy Hall of Fame, Oklahoma City.

DELBERT BUCK (b. 1976) is a self-taught Navajo sculptor and folk artist who achieved gallery representation at age fourteen. Uses found objects, carves and paints whimsical subjects in wood, particularly humorous and satirical renditions of popular subjects. Works collectively to construct art with family. Resides in New Mexico.

JULIE BUFFALOHEAD (b. 1972), Ponca, was born in Minneapolis, Minnesota. Earned B.F.A. from Minneapolis College of Art and Design, 1995; M.F.A. candidate, Cornell University. Works in mixed-media and collage. Resides in Ithaca, New York.

GEORGE ELBERT BURR (1859–1939) was born in Monroe Falls, Ohio. Studied briefly at Art Institute of Chicago. Was itinerant illustrator for *Harper's* and other magazines. Traveled in Europe. Became noted etcher, made more than 25,000. Moved to Denver in 1906, spent summers in Southwest deserts. Painted desert and Rocky Mountain scenes. Settled in Phoenix in 1924; died there.

DEBORAH BUTTERFIELD (b. 1949) was born in San Diego, California, received Master of Fine Arts degree, University of California, Davis, where trained in ceramics and sculpture. Sculpts horses in combinations of abstraction and realism. First worked in painted plaster over steel armatures, then used natural materials such as mud, branches, fibers. In 1980s, began using barbed wire, metal pipes, wood fencing, corrugated metal, chicken wire. Casts sculptures in bronze. Taught at University of Wisconsin, University of Montana. Raises horses on ranch in Bozeman, Montana.

In May 1861, **WILLIAM DE LA MONTAGNE CARY** (1840–1922) and two other New Yorkers went on excursion up Missouri River. Account of adventure "reads like the description of a boyhood idyll." They headed west; in Portland, Oregon, they boarded ship for San Francisco. Cary returned to New York via Panama Canal. Using sketches from this trip and one to Montana in 1874, had long career as western artist. In 1876, less than two weeks after the battle, painted earliest scene of battle on the Little Big Horn River, portrayed Custer as hero, creating enduring legend of Custer's "last stand." Died in Brookline, Massachusetts.

GERALD CASSIDY (1869–1934) was born in Covington, Kentucky, and raised in Cincinnati. Studied at Cincinnati Art Institute before briefly attending New York Art Students League and National Academy of Design in New York City. A successful commercial artist and lithographer, moved to Denver, then to Albuquerque, became illustrator. After moving to Santa Fe in 1915, sketched Pueblo Indians, landscapes, and murals. Died in Santa Fe when carbon monoxide fumes leaked from new gas heater in studio.

GEORGE CATLIN (1796–1872), born and raised on Wilkes Barre, Pennsylvania, farm, studied law but decided to become history painter. Studied briefly at Pennsylvania Academy, worked as portraitist. After seeing delegation of Indians in Philadelphia, decided to paint faithful renditions of North American Indians. In 1830, went to Saint Louis, painted portraits to earn money for trip up Missouri River. Eventually traveled entire western hemisphere from Alaska to Tierra del Fuego. Beginning in 1833, toured United States, Great Britain, and Europe with "Catlin's Indian Gallery" of more than six hundred portraits, landscapes, and genre scenes. Wrote and illustrated two-volume *Letters and Notes on the Manners, Customs, and Conditions of the North American Indians* (1841). Collection bought by businessman whose heirs donated it to Smithsonian Institution. Catlin spent last years at Smithsonian recreating earlier paintings. Died in Jersey City, New Jersey.

JEFFREY CHAPMAN (b. 1958), Anishnabe, was born in Minneapolis, Minnesota. Earned B.F.A, Minneapolis College of Art and Design, 1984. Painter and sculptor, best known for works on paper, particularly watercolor. Uses humor to explore dualities, identity, and balancing traditional beliefs with contemporary life. Constructs and demonstrates traditional Native American courting flute. Instructor of American Indian art history, Minneapolis (Minnesota) Community College.

Even as a child in his hometown of Ellensberg, Washington, **JOHN FORD CLYMER** (1907–1989) sketched incessantly; decided to become illustrator. After finishing high school enrolled at Vancouver (British Columbia) School of Art, supported himself by illustrating mail-order catalogs and magazines. Moved to Toronto to be near magazine publishers when twenty-one years old, but soon enrolled at Wilmington (Delaware) Academy of Art where he met prominent illustrator N. C. Wyeth. Returned to Canada for four years, then moved to New York City. Produced

scores of covers for *The Saturday Evening Post*. Wildlife and historical paintings allowed him to retire from illustrating and move to Teton Village, Wyoming. In 1974, won gold medal from National Academy of Western Art; in 1976 won its prestigious Prix de West.

Provo, Utah, native **MICHAEL COLEMAN** (b. 1946) works in gouache, the favorite medium of artist Henry Farny, a contemporary of Remington. As did Farny, Coleman portrays nineteenth-century Plains Indian life, painting in Farny's style.

Born in Portland, Maine, **SAMUEL COLMAN** (1832–1920) was among earliest independent artists to paint in the West. Concerned with effects of light and atmosphere. Made few, but evocative, images. Painting of Grand Canyon praised by critic in 1889 as example of ability to "reveal the glory and grandeur of the West."

Born in Springfield, Massachusetts, **HOWARD NORTON COOK** (1901–1980) attended New York Art Students League, studied with Andrew Dasburg and Maurice Sterne. From 1922 to 1925, traveled in Asia and Europe. In 1926, sent to New Mexico by *Forum* magazine. Traveled to Mexico in 1932 on Guggenheim Fellowship; studied fresco with assistant of Diego Rivera. Settled in Taos in 1935. Worked in many mediums into late 1970s. Died in Santa Fe.

ASTLEY DAVID MONTAGUE COOPER (1856–1924) was influenced by George Catlin, his mentor and friend. Attended Washington University in native Saint Louis, studied European art, portraiture, landscape drawing. At age twenty, traveled west in Catlin's footsteps, then worked as newspaper illustrator of Indians and Western landscapes. When twenty-four years old, established studio in San Francisco Latin Quarter. In 1883 moved to San Jose, California, was reputed to

pay bar bills with paintings of nudes. International reputation for romantic paintings of American Indians, buffalo herds portrayed in paradise lost. Legendary excesses better known than significant artistic achievements. Author of *Artists in California 1786–1940* declared Cooper most colorful of 16,000 artists chronicled. Accomplished violinist, played with local orchestras.

A native of northern mountain village of Cordova, New Mexico, woodcarver **GLORIA LOPEZ CORDOVA** (b. 1942) was first female *santera* (maker of religious images) in Cordova, ending male carving tradition established in 1920s by her grandfather, Jose Dolores Lopez. Exhibits frequently in Santa Fe Spanish Market. Winner of (New Mexico) Governor's Award for Excellence in the Arts, 2000.

At age sixteen, **EANGER IRVING COUSE** (1866–1936) left home in Saginaw, Michigan, to study at Art Institute of Chicago; moved to New York City, attended Art Students League, National Academy of Design. In 1886, enrolled at Academie Julian, Paris. Traveled West in 1891 to paint Indian subject for 1892 Paris Salon. After painting Native Americans in Northwest, visited Taos, New Mexico, in 1902, painted Taos Indians exclusively. After dividing time between Taos and New York for twenty-five years, moved to Taos in 1928. Elected to National Academy of Design in 1911; founding member and first president, Taos Society of Artists, 1915. Member, American Water Color Society, New York Water Color Club, and Society of Men Who Paint the Far West.

Ohioan **CHARLES CRAIG** (1846–1931) made first trip West in 1865, traveling up Missouri River. Studied at Philadelphia Academy of Fine Arts 1872–73. In 1881, sketched and painted in Taos, New Mexico, one of earliest artists to work there. Settled in Colorado Springs, Colorado, as first resident artist; for next fifty years painted, taught, and promoted other artists' work. Maintained nearly continuous exhibit in Antlers Hotel lobby; most paintings were lost in hotel fire in 1898.

EDWARD SHERIFF CURTIS (1868–1952) became photographer in his youth. After moving with his family to Seattle from birthplace, Whitewater, Wisconsin, photographed Indians in Puget Sound area; also became society photographer. In 1898, encouraged by Theodore Roosevelt and underwritten by J. Pierpont Morgan, began thirty-year project to photograph "all the important tribes of the United States and Alaska." Took tens of thousands of photographs for *The North American Indian*. Made portraits of individual Indians; cropped out signs of modernity. Worked for filmmaker Cecil B. DeMille in Los Angeles, where he died.

Born at San Ildefonso Pueblo, New Mexico, **POPOVI DA/ANTONIO MARTINEZ** (1921–1971) was son of renowned San Ildefonso potters Maria and Julian Martinez. Assisted family with pottery design. In addition to learning pottery-making at the pueblo, studied painting under Dorothy Dunn and Geronima Montoya at Santa Fe (New Mexico) Indian School. Practiced traditional Southwest-style of painting, best known for work with geometric designs and symbols.

CYRUS E. DALLIN (1861–1944) was born to pioneer parents in Springville, Utah Territory. Studied in East; established profitable studio. After attending Buffalo Bill Wild West show in Paris in 1889, became interested in Indians and horses as subjects, wished to portray "dignity typical of the Indian" in sculptures. Equestrian sculpture *Appeal to the Great Spirit* first shown at 1908 National Sculpture Society exhibition; awarded gold medal at 1909 Paris Salon.

Philadelphian **FELIX OCTAVIUS CARR DARLEY** (1822–1880) worked as illustrator, popularizing such American figures as the Pilgrim and the Pioneer. Made extensive illustrations for complete works of James Fenimore Cooper. Fame was so great that many books were advertised as being "illustrated by Darley." In 1849, moved to New York City hoping to increase his fame. In 1859, moved to Claymont, Delaware, resided at his studio, "The Wren's Nest." Was among such artists as Thomas Moran and Worthington Whittredge whose paintings, reproduced as engravings, were included in William Cullen Bryant's two-volume *Picturesque America*, published in 1872 and 1874. Darley influenced young Howard Pyle, who was seven years old when he moved to Delaware.

Photographer **DAVID DE HARPORT** (b. 1921) was born in Denver, Colorado, where he still lives. Began taking pictures while still in high school. First one-man show, Denver Art Mueum, Chappell House, 1942. Earned B. A., 1943, M.A., 1945, University of Denver. After publishing book of photographs of Colorado, won full-tuition scholarship to Harvard University, where earned M.A., 1949, Ph.D., 1960. Numerous awards and prestigious photographic assignments throughout career.

EDWIN WILLARD DEMING (1860–1942), born in Ashland, Ohio, grew up in frontier region of western Illinois. As youth, sketched Indians in Oklahoma. Studied at New York Art Students League and Academie Julian, Paris. Traveled in Southwest and Oregon, illustrating Sioux, Crow, Apache, and Pueblo Indians as individuals, not "ethnographic" types. Around 1900, series of murals of Indian life installed in American Museum of Natural History and Museum of the American Indian in New York.

MAMIE DESCHILLIE (b. 1920), Navajo, was born in Burnham, New Mexico. Self-taught folk artist. Specializes in mud toys and cardboard cut-out figures in traditional Navajo dress, both incorporating mixed media. Work exhibited in Museum of American Folk Art, New York, and internationally. Resides with extended family in New Mexico.

ALBERT DORNE (1904–1965) was born and grew up in New York City's lower east side. After eighth grade, left school to work. Was president, New York Society of Illustrators, 1947–48. In 1948, founded, directed Famous Artist School, Westport Connecticut. Noted for superb draftsmanship, compositional organization.

Westerner **HARVEY THOMAS DUNN** (1884–1952) was born in Manchester, South Dakota, but went east, joined elite "Brandywine School" of artists at Chadds Ford, Delaware, studied with illustrator Howard Pyle. Became leading illustrator for *The Saturday Evening Post*. Painted West of farmers and pioneers in tribute to his father, a "Dakota sod-buster." Taught illustration in New Jersey studio, emphasizing imaginative narrative skills.

In 1896, **WILLIAM HERBERT "BUCK" DUNTON** (1878–1936) left native Augusta, Maine, to work as ranch hand and hunter in Montana. For fifteen years, worked and hunted throughout West every summer, spent winters as illustrator in East. Moved to New York City in 1903; in 1911, enrolled in Art Students League; teacher Ernest Blumenschein encouraged him to visit Taos. Moved there in 1914. A founder of the Taos Society of Artists 1915, portrayed Anglo frontiersmen and pioneers. Died in Taos.

Coloradan **CHARLES R. C. "CHARLIE" DYE** (1906–1973) claimed he could not remember when he was not on horseback or sketching. In 1936 studied with Harvey Dunn in New York City. Became successful illustrator of the West, moved to Sedona, Arizona, in

1960. In 1964, Dye, Joe Beeler, and John Hampton founded Cowboy Artists of America "to perpetuate the memory and culture of the Old West."

Born in St. Louis, Missouri, **MICHAEL EASTMAN** (b. 1947) has worked for several decades as fine art and commercial photographer. Self-taught, he has been exhibited, published, and collected widely; has traveled on assignment throughout world.

A native of Brunswick, Maine, and graduate of West Point, where he studied and later taught topographical drawing, **SETH EASTMAN** (1808–1875) traveled west to serve with Army at Fort Snelling, Minnesota. Painted and photographed everyday life of Ojibwa (Chippewa) and Dakota (Sioux) tribes, Native Americans in Mississippi Valley. Opened Washington D.C. studio, specialized in Indian paintings drawn from memory and sketches.

A native of Gauting, Bavaria, where he saw films of Buffalo Bill's Wild West show, **NICK EGGENHOFER** (1897–1985) arrived in United States when sixteen years old. After studying at New York Cooper Union and American Lithographing Company, illustrated for numerous magazines; beginning in 1920, drew and painted covers for Western pulp fiction. Working from New Jersey studio, became noted for accurate renditions of early western vehicles. Moved to Cody, Wyoming, lived there for rest of his life.

HENRY FRANCOIS FARNY (1847–1916) was attracted to Indians in Warren, Pennsylvania, where his family immigrated from France in 1853. After family moved to Cincinnati, Ohio, began career as apprentice lithographer. Went to New York City in 1866 to work as engraver and cartoonist for *Harper's Monthly* magazine, then studied in Rome, Dusseldorf, and Munich. In 1870, returned to Cincinnati,

established studio. In 1881, traveled up Missouri River; sketched, took notes, collected Indian artifacts. Returned West between 1880 and 1900. Painted meticulously detailed, imaginative western scenes in gouache. Never visited Southwest, but illustrated Frank Cushing's memoir of life among the Zuni of New Mexico.

Cree Métis photographer and mixed-media artist **ROSALIE FAVELL** (b. 1958) was born in Winnipeg, Manitoba, Canada. Earned M.F.A., University of New Mexico, 1998. Her work addresses issues of gender and cultural identities, especially exploration of her experience as an urban and mixed-blood Indian. Works at White Mountain Academy of the Arts, Eliot Lake, Ontario, Canada.

Born in Kazan, Russia, **NICOLAI IVANOVICH FECHIN** (1881–1955) attended Kazan art school and Imperial Art Academy, Petrograd; became art instructor at Kazan art school. In 1913, exhibited at Carnegie Institute, Pittsburgh, Pennsylvania; in 1923, immigrated to New York City. Visited Taos, New Mexico, in 1926; moved there, 1927, became American citizen, 1931. In 1933, moved to Santa Monica, California. Died in Santa Monica studio.

Austrian **JOSEPH AMADEUS FLECK** (1893–1977) studied at Royal Viennese Art Academy and Royal Art Academy, Munich. Immigrated to United States, 1922. Settled in Taos, mid-1920s, became American citizen. Painted Taos landscape, Indians. In 1942, named Dean of Fine Arts, University of Missouri, Kansas City. Returned to Taos in 1946; shortly before death moved to Pleasanton, California.

POLLY ROSE FOLWELL/QUAH-EH/LITTLE RAIN (b. 1962), Santa Clara, learned traditional pottery techniques from grandmother, Rose Naranjo, and mother, Jody Folwell. Participant in Indian Market, Santa Fe, New Mexico, since 1978.

Winona, Minnesota, native **JAMES EARLE FRASER** (1876–1953) went to Paris in 1898 to study with master sculptor Augustus Saint-Gaudens. In 1907, became sculpture instructor at New York Art Students League; established studio in Greenwich Village. Went West with family in 1880. After sculpture, *End of the Trail*, won gold medal at 1915 Panama-Pacific International Exposition, San Francisco, became perhaps most popular sculptor in America. Sold rights to *End of the Trail* to silverware and china manufacturers. In 1951, won Gold Medal for Sculpture from American Academy of Arts and Letters.

Sculptor **EDWARD JAMES FRAUGHTON** (b. 1939) was born in Park City, Utah; received B. F. A. University of Utah, 1962. Member, National Sculpture Society, Utah Westerners. Lives in South Jordan, Utah.

In 1873, *Harper's Weekly* commissioned French artists **PAUL FRENZENY** (c. 1840–1902) and Jules Tavernier to make sketches while crossing country from New York City to San Francisco through Southwest. Frenzeny remained in San Francisco, became active member of Bohemian Club and artists' colony. In 1878, returned to New York City. In 1880s, illustrated for *Harper's* and other magazines. After creating more than one hundred illustrations for Harrington O'Reilly's *Fifty Years on the Trail; A True Story of Western Life*, dropped completely from view.

VIRGINIA GARCIA (b. 1963), San Juan and Santa Clara, was born in Santa Fe, New Mexico, into family of accomplished potters. Ceramicist known for exploring and refining traditional Santa Clara pottery, in undecorated, elegant forms. Exhibits in Santa Fe Indian Market and contemporary art gallery.

MARCO ANTONIO "TONY" GOMEZ (1910–1972) was born in Durango, Mexico. Pupil of father, famous Mexican portraitist who moved with family to Arizona in 1918. Studied at Chouinard's Art Center in Los Angeles. Official artist, 433rd Fighter Squadron, World War II. Painted Old West exclusively. Died in Manhattan, Beach, California.

Born in Norwich, Connecticut, **PHILLIP RUSSELL GOODWIN** (1881–1935) spent his boyhood sketching; sold first illustrated story to *Collier's* magazine when eleven. Became student of Howard Pyle at Brandywine School, Chadds Ford, Pennsylvania, when seventeen, was classmate of N.C. Wyeth and Frank Schoonover. Later attended Rhode Island School of Design. Member, New York Art Students League. Became friends of Carl Rungius and Charles Russell when all had studios in New York City. Spent many summers in West including time with Russell on his ranch in Kalispell, Montana. Illustrated many books and magazines. Died of pneumonia in Mamaroneck, New York, studio.

ARTHUR WILLIAM HALL (1889–1981) was born in Bowie, Texas. Studied at Art Institute of Chicago and in Scotland. Etcher, also made dry points and aquatints of southwestern subjects. In 1940s moved to Santa Fe, New Mexico, occupied Gerald Cassidy's studio. Moved to Alcalde. Spent final years in Sun City, Arizona.

Inspired by George Catlin's art and James Fenimore Cooper's stories, **HERMAN WENDLEBORG HANSEN** (1854–1924) immigrated from Dithmarschen, Germany, 1877. Trained in Hamburg and London, worked as commercial artist in New York City and Chicago. Traveled to Dakotas to sketch Indians and buffalo. Studied at Art Institute of Chicago. Settled permanently in San Francisco. Never an illustrator, made frequent sketching tours of Southwest and Mexico; "prime motif" was the horse. Most paintings and Native American artifacts destroyed in 1906 San Francisco earthquake. In 1924, took

up etching; created several successful works before his death.

JOHN HAUSER (1858 or 1859–1913) returned to his native Cincinnati, Ohio, to launch art career after study in Munich and Dusseldorf, Germany, and Paris. Traveled in New Mexico and Arizona; specialized in painting Indians.

Chippewa and Choctaw painter **JAMES HAVARD** (b. 1937) was born in Galveston, Texas. Earned B.S., Sam Houston State College, Huntsville, Texas, 1959; attended Atelier Chapman Kelly, Dallas, Texas, 1960; Pennsylvania Academy of Fine Arts, Philadelphia, Pennsylvania, 1965. Works in oil and acrylic in style he defines as "abstract illusionism." Resides in Philadelphia, Pennsylvania.

EARLE ERIK HEIKKA (1910–1941) was born in Belt, Montana, to Finnish immigrant parents and grew up in Great Falls. As child, modeled animals from clay; by time he was eighteen, made animals of wood, leather, cloth, papier mâché, plastic, and metal. Most work featured pack trains, stagecoaches, cowboys, and Indians; few models had been cast in bronze at time of his mysterious death from bullet wound.

ERNEST MARTIN HENNINGS (1886–1956) was born in Penns Grove, New Jersey, raised in Chicago. Graduated from Chicago Art Institute, 1904, worked as illustrator. In 1912 studied at Munich's Royal Academy. Returned to Chicago in 1915; went to New Mexico in 1917; in 1921, made Taos permanent home. Joined Taos Society of Artists, 1924. During the 1920s won several major prizes. Received last large commission in 1955 from Santa Fe Railway to paint on Navajo Reservation. Died in Taos home.

Next to Albert Bierstadt, **THOMAS HILL** (1829–1908) was most famous member of "California School" of landscape painters.

Began career as decorative painter in Boston after training in Europe. Also member of "Rocky Mountain School," which included Bierstadt and Thomas Moran. Settled in northern California, was interested in effects of light. Became best known for paintings of Yosemite. Hill's monumental 1881 painting, *Driving the Last Spike*, commemorating the completion of the first transcontinental railroad at Promontory Point, Utah, hangs in the California State Capitol in Sacramento.

New Yorker **RANSOM GILLET HOLDREDGE** (1836–1899) went to San Francisco, worked as draftsman, studied with local artists, exhibited popular landscapes painted in Hudson River style. Field artist for *Scribner's* with Army troops at time of battle of the Little Big Horn. Sketched throughout West, painted seascapes, Indians in mountain landscapes. Died in Alameda, California.

Warm Springs Chiricahua Apache artist **ALLAN HOUSER/HAOZOUS** (1914–1994) was born in Apache, Oklahoma, shortly after his family's tribe was released from twenty-seven years' detention by U.S. Government. Studied with Dorothy Dunn at Santa Fe (New Mexico) Indian School, 1934–39. Painter and highly regarded and influential sculptor, known for both abstract and representational work. Taught at Institute of American Indian Arts, Santa Fe, 1962–75. Awarded National Medal of Arts in 1992.

PETER HURD (1904–1984) was born in San Patricio, New Mexico. While a West Point cadet, sold painting to supervisor, decided to become artist rather than career soldier. Enrolled in Pennsylvania Academy of the Fine Arts in 1924, also took lessons from illustrator N.C. Wyeth. In 1929, began to work in egg tempera on panel. After marrying Wyeth's daughter Henriette, returned to New Mexico; both became well-known artists. Completed several murals in mid-1930s for

Federal Arts Project. Painted landscapes and genre paintings with atmospheric quality typical of Southwest light and color.

Born in Tulsa, Oklahoma, **WILSON HURLEY** (b. 1924) attended high school in New Mexico, visited Santa Fe artists Theodore Van Soelen and Jozef Bakos. Attended U.S. Military Academy; was WWII pilot. Earned law degree from George Washington University, Washington, D.C.; practiced for several years. In 1964, became full-time painter; in 1996, completed fifteen dioramas of sunsets in famous American landmarks such as Grand Canyon and Yellowstone National Park. Lives in Albuquerque, New Mexico.

Brooklyn, New York, native **JOSEPH A. IMHOF** (1871–1955) studied in Brussels, Paris, and Munich before arriving in the Southwest in 1904. A self-taught lithographer, after settling in Taos specialized in painting New Mexico landscape.

Wyoming sculptor **HARRY JACKSON** (b. 1924) created well-known sculpture of John Wayne installed on Wilshire Boulevard in Hollywood, California. Celebrates mythology of Old West in sculpture based on "elemental schemes." Born in Chicago, went west to work as cowboy. Moving to New York in 1946, became devotee of abstract expressionist artist Jackson Pollock; eventually gave up career as abstract painter to become realist painter and sculptor. His monumental sculpture *Sacajawea* at Buffalo Bill Historical Center in Cody, Wyoming, is among best-known works.

Photographer **WILLIAM HENRY JACKSON** (1843–1942) first went west in 1866. After adventures as teamster and "trail-riding vaquero," moved to Omaha, bought photography studio. Invited by Ferdinand V. Hayden to join U.S. Geological and Geographical Survey of the Territories in 1871 to source of the Yellowstone River as official photographer. Was first to photograph region. Collaborated with painter Thomas Moran to create powerful photographic and painted images of Yellowstone. Continued to accompany Hayden's surveys. In 1873, took first photograph of famous Mountain of the Holy Cross in Colorado Rockies; in 1876, Jackson's photograph and Moran's painting of "The Mount of the Holy Cross" were wildly popular attractions at Philadelphia Centennial Exposition.

DOUGLAS JOHNSON (b. 1946) was born in Portland, Oregon. A self-taught artist, lives in Coyote, New Mexico, paints in gouache and makes pottery.

FRANK TENNEY JOHNSON (1874–1939) was New York illustrator when he moved to California in 1920s to paint cowboys, settlers, and Indians. Member of informal group of California illustrators such as Edward Borein and Maynard Dixon, became noted for night scenes of the Santa Fe Trail. His illustrations were used as cover art for several books by western novelist Zane Grey.

Austrian watchmaker **CARL KAUBA** (1865–1922) studied art at Vienna academies. May have visited the United States in 1880s. His bronzes were cast in Vienna from models based on photographs, illustrations, and American artifacts. Many bronzes exported to the United States between 1895–1912.

Born in Hagerstown, Maryland, **JOHN ROSS KEY** (1832–1920), grandson of Francis Scott Key, studied art in Munich and Paris, established studio in Boston, then in Chicago. Perfected drawing, mapmaking skills while draftsman for U.S. Coast and Geodetic Survey. In 1869, moved to San Francisco to paint landscapes of Yosemite, Tahoe, Point Lobos, and other California landmarks. Won gold medal at 1876 Philadelphia Centennial Exposition.

GENE KLOSS (1903–1996) was born Alice Geneva Glasier in Oakland, California. After marriage to poet Phillips Kloss in 1925, called herself Gene Kloss. Graduated from University of California at Berkeley, 1924; studied at California School of Fine Arts, San Francisco, and College of Arts and Crafts, Oakland. First visited New Mexico on honeymoon; took along etching press, worked at campsite in Taos Canyon. In 1929, established permanent Taos studio but returned to Berkeley every winter. In 1933–34, worked for WPA as etcher, her principal medium. Between 1924 and 1985, completed more than 600 etchings. After 1985, quit etching but completed editions of some earlier plates until failing health forced her to stop.

WILLIAM (WILHELM) HEINRICH DETLEV (W. H. D.) KOERNER (1878–1938) was born in Germany, grew up in Clinton, Iowa, on west bank of Mississippi River. Studied art briefly in Clinton, became staff artist for *Chicago Tribune*. Went West for first time in 1924, drove 5,000 miles in Buick touring car. In 1927, visited Southwest. Moved to New York City, studied at Art Students League, then Brandywine School, Chadds Ford, Delaware, with Howard Pyle. Tall man, known as "Big Bill," was never easel painter; instead, became regular illustrator for *The Saturday Evening Post*, specializing in western scenes. Produced more than two thousand illustrations.

CORNELIUS DAVID KRIEGHOFF (1815–1872) was born and studied art in Dusseldorf, Germany; also trained as professional musician. Traveled through Europe as itinerant artist-musician. Immigrated to United States, 1837, joined Army of invasion against Seminole Indians in Florida. After discharge, opened studio in Rochester, New York; later settled in Quebec. Became one of most important Canadian painters. Painted Indians at daily tasks. In 1868, moved to Chicago, where he died.

SYDNEY LAURENCE(1865–1940) was first professionally trained artist to live in Alaska. Brooklyn native, studied at New York Art Students League. In 1889, moved to art colony at St. Ives, Cornwall, England, exhibited at Royal Society of British Artists. Included in Paris Salons of 1890, 1894, 1895. Moved to Alaska in 1904 to be prospector. In 1911, began again to make art, settled in Anchorage in 1915. By early 1920s was Alaska's best-known painter. From mid-1920s until his death, spent summers in Alaska, winters in the Lower Forty-eight. Mt. McKinley was favorite subject. Credited with defining Alaskan landscape for painters who followed.

WILLIAM ROBINSON LEIGH (1866–1955) was an eager convert to Thomas Moran's philosophy that an artist "should paint his own land." Born on West Virginia farm, drew animals at early age. When only twelve, won award from Washington, D.C. art collector, W. W. Corcoran, for drawing of dog. Studied at Maryland Institute of Art, Baltimore; went to Munich for more training. Was well-known illustrator in 1897 when *Scribner's Magazine* sent him to North Dakota on his first trip west. Wanting to be fine artist rather than illustrator, in 1906 persuaded Santa Fe Railway to send him west in return for painting of Grand Canyon. His ability to portray horses and other animals with absolute accuracy made him much-sought-after western painter.

CARM LITTLE TURTLE (b. 1952) was born in Santa Maria, California. Apache and Tarahumara descent, she attended College of the Redwoods, Eureka, California, 1980, University of New Mexico, 1978–79. A photographer and mixed media artist, hand-painted black and white or sepia-toned photographs are her hallmark. Narrative subjects include relationships to land, identity issues in art world, and interpersonal relationships. Works as registered nurse, lives in Bosque Farms, New Mexico.

Ho-chunk artist TRUMAN LOWE (b. 1944) was born in Black River Falls, Wisconsin. Earned M.F.A. from University of Wisconsin, Madison, 1973. Received Eiteljorg Fellowship for Native American Fine Art, 1999. Sculptor, printmaker, works with mixed-media to explore natural forms using materials from the environment such wood and feathers. Abstractly interprets natural elements, especially water, illuminating his connection to land and Woodlands traditions. Works as art instructor and curator.

Watsonville, California, native BRUCE LOWNEY (b. 1937) received a B.A. in Fine Arts and English Literature, North Texas State University, and an M.A. in printmaking and art history from San Francisco State University; studied lithography at University of New Mexico. Lives in New Mexico.

JUDITH LOWRY (b. 1948), of Mountain Maidu, Hamowi Pit River, and Euro-Australian descent, was born in Washington, D.C. Earned M.A., Chico State University. As member of an army family, as a child she traveled widely in United States and abroad. Large-scale paintings reflect influence of Italian Renaissance and narrative Native American traditions. Explores themes of cultural stereotypes, contemporary Indian life, mixed-blood heritage and family stories. Lives with family in Nevada City, California.

JOHN NORVAL MARCHAND (1875–1921) was born in Leavenworth, Kansas, became western painter and sculptor. Studied at Harwood Art School, Minneapolis. Staff artist, *New York World*. In 1897–99, studied at Munich Academy. Returned to New York City, worked as illustrator. Made sketching trips west. Met Charles Russell in Montana, 1902; hosted him in New York City. Died in Westport, Connecticut.

GEORGE B. MARKS (b. 1923) grew up on Iowa farm, began art studies at University of Iowa, received B. A. Degree, 1950. Held summer job in Yellowstone National Park, saw Charlie Russell's work, which inspired him to paint the West. Moved to Albuquerque, New Mexico.

MARIA MARTINEZ (c. 1887–1980), San Ildefonso, was innovative ceramicist who, with husband Julian Martinez (1887–1943), revolutionized Pueblo ceramics in early 20th century. Their revival of traditional firing techniques and creation of enormously successful black-on-black ware were integral to advancement of commercial pottery industry and recognition of the craft as art. After Julian's death, Maria worked with daughter-in-law Santana and other relatives. Work highly valued in museum collections throughout world.

Yaqui artist MARIO MARTINEZ (b. 1953) was born in Phoenix, Arizona. Earned B.F.A., Arizona State University, 1979; M.F.A., San Francisco Art Institute, 1985. Influence of European modernist traditions in printmaking, drawings, large-scale paintings, and murals. Uses abstraction to depict Yaqui concepts and beliefs. Taught at Institute of American Indian Arts, Santa Fe, New Mexico, 1991–92. Lives in San Francisco.

Navajo ceramicist CHRISTINE NOFCHISSEY McHORSE (b. 1948) was born in Morenci, Arizona. Attended Institute of American Indian Arts, High School program, Santa Fe, New Mexico, 1963–67. Learned pottery techniques from mother-in-law Priscilla Namingha, Taos Pueblo. Specializes in elegant hand-built pots using micaceous clay from Taos region; works in jewelry. Frequent participant and award winner, Santa Fe Indian Market. Lives in New Mexico.

ALFRED JACOB MILLER (1810–1874) was born in Baltimore, Maryland. Studied at

Ecole des Beaux-Arts, Paris; toured Italy, 1833–34. Returned to Baltimore, then opened studio in New Orleans. Commissioned by Scottish baronet Sir William Drummond Stewart to accompany six-month expedition to Rocky Mountains. Spent summer of 1837 with fur traders traveling from Saint Louis to trappers' annual "rendezvous" in what is now Wyoming. Became only artist to paint mountain men and trappers from life, creating the West's first authentic hero. Following expedition, returned to New Orleans, painted eighteen large oils and nearly two hundred watercolors from sketches. Returned to Baltimore, exhibited first views of Rockies ever seen in the East. Spent rest of life painting western scenes he had painted for Stewart.

N. Scott Momaday (b. 1934), Kiowa, was born in Lawton, Oklahoma. B.A., University of New Mexico, 1958; M.A., Stanford University, 1960; Ph.D., 1963. Best known as poet and author, also works in acrylic, watercolor, pen and ink, pastel, and printmaking. Resides in Tucson, Arizona.

Peter Moran (1841–1914) was youngest of four Moran brothers. Family immigrated to United States from England in 1844. Was apprenticed to lithographer when sixteen years old, then studied with brothers Thomas and Edward. Maintained studio in Philadelphia for remainder of career. Traveled to New Mexico, 1864, early 1880s. Made trips west with brothers. In 1890, one of five artists sent west by U.S. Census Bureau to take 1890 census among Indians. Report contained his illustrations of Indians. Died in Philadelphia.

When he first traveled west, **Thomas Moran** (1837–1926) was Philadelphia engraver and painter. Born in Lancashire, England, came with family to United States in 1844. Apprenticed to engraver but preferred painting and sketching mythological scenes. Felt that painting American landscape was his destiny. Paintings appeared authentic but he sought "higher truth." Made first western landscapes at Green River, Wyoming, in 1871, while traveling to meet U. S. Geological Survey expedition to Yellowstone country.

Alfred Gwynne Morang (1901–1958) was born in Ellsworth, Maine. Uncle provided painting and music lessons; by teens, supported himself playing and teaching violin. At age sixteen, began to study painting with impressionist artists who summered in Maine. Also became well-known short-story writer, had fellowship at Yaddo, Saratoga Springs, New York. Tuberculosis sent him to Santa Fe, New Mexico, for healthful climate. Impressionist painter, also wrote, taught art. Died in studio fire.

Hopi and Zuni ceramicist **Les Namingha** (b. 1967) was born in Zuni, New Mexico. Earned B.A. in design, Brigham Young University, 1992. Learned traditional pottery-making techniques from Hopi aunt, Dextra Nampeyo. Combines traditional and contemporary design in work.

Philadelphia-born painter **Willard Ayer Nash** (1898–1943) studied art in Detroit, traveled to Santa Fe, 1920. Studied modernist techniques with Andrew Dasburg, who introduced him to work of Cezanne, influenced New Mexico landscapes. Cofounder of Santa Fe artist group Los Cinco Pintores. In 1936, left Santa Fe for California, taught in San Francisco and Los Angeles.

Born in Sweden, **B.J.O. Nordfeldt** (1878–1955) immigrated to Chicago in 1891. Studied at Art Institute, 1899. After studying art for decade in Chicago and Europe, moved to Santa Fe in 1919, remained next twenty years. Influence of Cezanne and the Fauves apparent in landscapes and portraits.

Janice Ortiz (b. 1956), Cochiti, was born in California. Member of pottery-making family in Cochiti Pueblo, New Mexico, began making pottery when only twelve years old. Contemporary interpretation of pueblo figurative tradition, including storytellers and playful parodies of non-Indians. Exhibits in Santa Fe Indian Market and in numerous galleries. Works as public school teacher, Albuquerque, New Mexico.

William Andrew Pacheco (b. 1975), Santo Domingo, attended New Mexico State University, 1994–97; University of New Mexico, 1997–2000. Member of Tenoria family of potters at Santo Domingo Pueblo, New Mexico. Began training when just ten years old, working in traditional designs and forms; later added dinosaurs to repertoire.

Edgar Samuel Paxson (1852–1919) was born near Buffalo, New York, grew up with love of the West. Displayed artistic talent through school years. When twenty years old, traveled to Midwest and California, carrying art supplies in his saddlebags; seldom returned east. In 1879, settled in Montana, became landscape and sign painter. Best known for painting of Battle of the Little Bighorn, *Custer's Last Stand.*

George Phippen (1916–1966) was raised on midwestern farms; as child, sketched animals. After WWII, moved to Santa Fe, studied with Henry Balink, worked as commercial artist and illustrator. Began making cowboy art in late 1950s, was first president of Cowboy Artists of America.

Lillian Pitt (b. 1943), Wasco, Warm Springs, and Yakama, was born in Warm Springs, Oregon. Largely self-taught sculptor, known for hand-built masks in early career, as well as work in mixed media, jewelry, clay, and bronze. Celebrates ancient beliefs and forms, including petroglyph imagery from

Plateau region. Themes of healing and transformation appear throughout work. Retrospective exhibition at Warm Springs Museum, 1999. Participated in cultural exchanges with Japanese paper-maker and artists from Pacific Northwest. Owns gallery and works in Portland, Oregon.

OGDEN MINTON PLEISSNER (1905–1983) was born in Brooklyn, New York, graduated from Brooklyn Friends School, 1922; studied at New York Art Students League, 1923–27. Taught at Pratt Institute, 1930–34, then at National Academy. In 1936, opened studio in Manhattan; remained there for forty years. Elected Associate in National Academy, 1937; Academician, 1940. After serving in Army Air Force during World War II, served as war correspondent for Life magazine, 1944–45. In 1977, moved to Vermont. Traveled and painted through Europe. Died in London.

ALEXANDER PHIMISTER PROCTOR (1862–1950) was born in Ontario, Canada, and raised in Denver, Colorado. As youth, trekked through forests, hunted big game. Studied at New York Art Students League and National Academy of Design, 1888. In 1891, made decorative sculpture for Chicago Columbian Exposition; produced more than thirty-five models of wild animals of America including moose, elk, mountain lion. Two equestrian statues—a cowboy and an Indian scout—stood in Exposition. After study in Paris in 1893, returned to New York City to model equestrian statues for Central Park; returned to Paris for further study. Elected Associate in National Academy, 1900. Reopened New York City studio. Made bronzes of animals for Bronx Zoo and entrance to Brooklyn's Prospect Park; sculpted tigers for Princeton University; they won gold medal from Architectural League of New York. In 1914 headed west. Last major work, *Monument to the Mustangs*, was unveiled at University of Texas, Austin, two years before his death.

When he was a young boy, **HENRY RASCHEN** (1856–1938) and his family immigrated from Germany to northern California. Studied at San Francisco Art Association, then in Munich. Traveled in Italy and France. For eight years, traveled among California Indian tribes, became Indian painter. Oakland, California, his final home. Member of San Francisco Art Association and Bohemian Club.

In 1940s and 1950s, **DOEL REED** (1895–1985) was internationally known printmaker. Born in rural Indiana, was raised in Indianapolis. Studied at Cincinnati Art Academy. In 1924 became first artist to teach on faculty of Oklahoma A & M College. Retired in 1959, moved to Taos, where he had summered since 1940s. Was elected to National Academy, 1952.

It is believed that **LEONARD HOWARD REEDY** (1899–1956) was born and died in Chicago. Spent much time as youth working as ranch hand in West. Known as Chicago's "Cowboy Painter" of Old West, studied at Art Institute and Chicago Academy of Fine Arts.

Primarily an illustrator and painter, **FREDERIC REMINGTON** (1861–1909) turned to sculpture late in career. Born in Canton, New York, grew up in Ogdensburg. In 1881, went to Montana Territory. Decided to become artist, attended New York Art Students League. Made short trips West to collect information and inspiration; completed art works in New York studio. Rendered universal types, larger than life, to represent West. First western illustration commission from *Harper's Weekly*; work appeared in *Harper's* through 1880s–90s. Illustrated Theodore Roosevelt's articles about life among cowboys. In 1891, settled in New Rochelle, New York. Began to produce sculpture, "the most perfect expression of action." *Bronco Buster* was first bronze; more than two hundred were cast. By 1907, had produced many sculptures, including *The Rattlesnake* and *The Outlaw*. While on visit

to Southwest, decided never to go west again as it was "too civilized." Died of acute appendicitis.

Ohioan **CLEVELAND SALTER ROCKWELL** (1837–1907) may have received art training in New York City, but was mostly self-taught. Documented Pacific Northwest coast. In 1856, appointed to U.S. Coast Survey; worked with Survey for two decades while living in Portland, Oregon. Retired from survey, 1892; continued to paint until death. Produced comprehensive views of Pacific Northwest waterways, especially Columbia and Willamette Rivers; included Native Americans fishing or boating.

Born in New York City, **NORMAN PERCEVEL ROCKWELL** (1894–1978) was a popular illustrator known for his *Saturday Evening Post* covers. Portrayed everyday "life as I would like it to be." In 1908, began studies at Chase School of Fine and Applied Art, New York City; quit high school to study at National Academy of Design, New York Art Students League. Illustrated first book in 1911; in 1913 became illustrator, art director for *Boys Life* magazine. In 1915, moved to artist colony in New Rochelle, New York, to be near other illustrators. In 1916, sold first illustrations to editor of *The Saturday Evening Post*, beginning four-decade relationship; produced more than three hundred covers. In 1923, went to Paris to become modern artist but returned to illustration, accepting book commissions. Moved to Vermont, 1939. In 1953, moved to Stockbridge, Massachusetts, remained there for rest of life.

Cochiti artist **DIEGO ROMERO** (b. 1964) was born in Berkeley, California. Attended Institute of American Indian Arts, Santa Fe, New Mexico, 1986. Earned B.F.A., Otis-Parsons Art Institute, Los Angeles, 1990; M.F.A., University of California, Los Angeles, 1993. Ceramicist known for contemporary interpretation of ancient Mimbres forms; also painter and printmaker. Explores diverse subjects, from traditional and contemporary Indian cultural and political issues to Greek mythology. Resides in New Mexico.

CARL CLEMENS MORITZ RUNGIUS (1869–1959) was born in Berlin, Germany. Grandson of taxidermist and wild-game hunter; drew animals. First visited United States in 1894; the following year hunted in Wyoming. Settled on Long Island, New York, 1897, spent summers hunting in West. Began visiting Alberta, Canada, in 1910; in 1921, built home and studio in Banff; spent summers there until 1958. Wildlife painter and sculptor. Theodore Roosevelt collected his work.

Known as the "Cowboy Artist," **CHARLES MARION RUSSELL** (1864–1926) was born in suburban Saint Louis. Traveled to Montana in 1880 to work on sheep ranch, first of several jobs as hunter, trapper, ranch wrangler. Steeped in elements that would appear in his art works, particularly cowboy and Indian life. Sketched and drew as youth, was self-taught. First art work believed to be small wax sculpture of horse. When sixteen, moved to Montana, determined to become artist. First major oil, *Breaking Camp* (1885). In 1904, cast *Smoking Up* in bronze; it was immediate success. After 1907, exhibited in New York City, spent part of each winter in southern California. From 1900, permanent home in Great Falls, Montana, where he died.

ANTON SCHONBORN (d. 1871) immigrated to the United States from Germany, became survey topographical artist. Traveled with 1859 expedition to upper Yellowstone River; in 1871 joined survey of Yellowstone basin with W. H. Jackson, photographer, and Thomas Moran, who went as guest. Best known for depictions of western forts.

FRANK EARLE SCHOONOVER (1878–1972) was born in New Jersey, lived in Pennsylvania, studied with Howard Pyle at Brandywine School, Chadds Ford, Delaware. Illustrated books and magazines, illustrated own stories. By 1930s, made transition to easel painting, completed more than four thousand paintings, many of lone figures involved in a challenge or struggle; preferred ideals types to individual portraits.

ARTHUR SCHOTT (1813–1875) accompanied United States–Mexico boundary survey from 1849–55, drew, painted regional flora and fauna for three-volume report of expedition published in 1857–59. Ardent naturalist, after survey resided in Washington; city directory listed him as naturalist, engineer, physician, and professor of German and music.

Along with Remington and Russell, **CHARLES SCHREYVOGEL** (1861–1912) was best-known painter of the West. Born in New York City, showed artistic talent while still young boy; was apprenticed to engraver. Studied in Munich. Dreamed of American West after attending 1887 performance of Buffalo Bill Wild West show; in 1893, spent summer on Ute reservation in southwestern Colorado. Made sketches, photographs, collected Native artifacts and western firearms, which he took to studio in Hoboken, New Jersey. In 1900, *My Bunkie* won cash prize in National Academy of Fine Arts annual exhibition. Elected Associate in National Academy of Design, 1901. Created visual history of Army of the West, 1860s–80s. *The Last Drop* is among few models later cast in bronze. After Remington's death, was declared "America's greatest living interpreter of the Old West." Died of blood poisoning in Hoboken.

OLAF CARL BORRE SELTZER (1877–1957) was born in Copenhagen, Denmark, attended Technical Institute of Copenhagen when twelve years old. Immigrated with wid-

owed mother to Montana when fourteen. Became machinist in Great Northern Railroad shops, met Charles Russell, who taught him and remained lifelong friend. Went to New York, 1926–27, after Russell's death, to complete some of his commissions; returned to Great Falls, Montana, painted more than 2,500 western scenes. Died in Great Falls.

SAMUEL SEYMOUR (1775–after 1823) was first artist to paint trans-Mississippi West. Traveled with Stephen H. Long's expedition across Plains to Front Range of Rockies in 1819–20. Considered an "elusive character," was known to be living in New York City, 1823. Made first sketch of Kansas, *War Dance in the Interior of a Konza Lodge*, drawn near the site of Manhattan in 1819.

Born in Bridgeport, Ohio, **JOSEPH HENRY SHARP** (1859–1953) began art lessons when fourteen years old. In 1881, made first of three trips to study art in Europe. Traveled West in 1883, sketched Indians in Pacific Northwest; Indians became principal subject. Went to Taos, New Mexico, 1893. At Academie Julian, Paris, in 1895, told art students Ernest Blumenschein and Bert Phillips about Taos, leading them to establish Taos art colony in 1898. Went to Montana to paint Plains Indians in 1899. In 1909, established Taos studio; in 1915 became founding member of Taos Society of Artists. In 1920s bought winter home in Pasadena, California; traveled to Hawaii.

HENRY MERWIN SHRADY (1871–1922) was born in New York City, studied law at Columbia University, but was too ill to practice. In 1900, began drawing and painting. Sculptor Karl Bitter saw him sketching at zoo, offered studio space. Became successful sculptor. Died in New York.

WILLIAM HOWARD SHUSTER (1893–1969) was born in Philadelphia, Pennsylvania, studied at Drexel Institute. After serving in U.S. Army, WWI, contracted tuberculosis, moved to Santa Fe for health in 1920. Member of Santa Fe painters' group, Los Cinco Pintores. Close friend of New York artist John Sloan who summered in Santa Fe. In 1930s, as New Deal artist, painted murals and easel paintings, notably, Indian subjects. Died in Santa Fe.

Navajo painter and printmaker **ED SINGER** (b. 1951) was born in Tuba City, Arizona. Primarily self-taught, also earned B.F.A., San Francisco Art Institute; attended University of Northern Arizona, 1973–76. Specializes in two-dimensional work, including paint, pastel, lithography and mixed media. Known for dynamic, gestural images of contemporary Navajo subjects, especially cowboys. Resides in Bosque Farms, New Mexico.

Born in Lock Haven, Pennsylvania, **JOHN SLOAN** (1871–1951) began career as newspaper artist in Philadelphia while studying at Pennsylvania Academy of the Fine Arts. Followed teacher Robert Henri to New York City in 1904. Became member of The Eight, also known as Ash Can School. Was in 1913 Armory Show. Taught at Art Students League, was editor of *The Masses*. Visited Santa Fe in 1919; established home, returned every summer, where his palette brightened in response to light and color. Painted landscapes and scenes of southwestern life while promoting exhibitions of Native American art in the East.

JOHN C. SMART (b. 1947) is a Montana photographer. In 1969, traveled to India and Nepal. Trip inspired him to study photography at Chicago Art Institute. In early 1970s, adopted 4 x 5 inch format camera and black and white print. Drawn to Montana where he could "grasp in a single sweeping glance a vision of the earth as a living organism." Settled there in 1977.

Flathead artist **JAUNE QUICK-TO-SEE SMITH** (b. 1940) was born at St. Ignatius, on Flathead Indian Reservation. Earned M.A., University of New Mexico, 1980. Received Eiteljorg Fellowship for Native American Fine Art, 1999. Internationally renowned, addresses environmental and identity issues. Abstract and expressive paintings incorporate collage and text. Has worked as advocate for Native issues and contemporary Native American artists throughout career. Resides in Corrales, New Mexico.

JOHN MIX STANLEY (1814–1872) had little formal training, first saw West in 1846 as artist for Army of the West during Mexican War. In 1853, accompanied Pacific Railway Survey searching for most feasible route for transcontinental railroad. Painted Indian Gallery, most of which burned in fire at Smithsonian Institution in 1865. Composed paintings to valorize Indians and Indian life.

DOROTHY NEWKIRK STEWART (1891–1955) was born in Philadelphia, Pennsylvania, studied at Philadelphia Academy of Fine Arts and University of Pennsylvania. Authored nonfiction books on Southwest and Mexico. Joined Santa Fe art colony around 1925. Traveled in Mexico, 1930s–50s. Converted car to "covered wagon," went on painting excursions around New Mexico. Opened Galeria Mexico as gallery and printmaking studio. Published her hand-painted editions of works of Shakespeare and other volumes, including *Handbook of Indian Dances*. Died in Mexico.

Born near Liverpool, England, **ARTHUR FITZWILLIAM TAIT** (1819–1905) was a self-taught painter who immigrated to New York in 1850. Master of detailed, realistic paintings. Elected to full membership in National Academy of Design, 1858. Specialized in hunting and sporting scenes set in American West and Adirondack Mountains of upstate New York. Never traveled west of

Chicago; relied on work of other artists for critical information.

LUIS TAPIA (b. 1950) was born in Santa Fe, New Mexico. Self-taught, works as sculptor, painter, often of Hispanic religious art. Cofounder, La Cofradia de Artes y Artesanos Hispanicos. Exhibited in *Santos, Statues and Sculpture: Contemporary Wood Carving from New Mexico*, 1988; *Hispanic Art in the United States*, 1989.

CHRISTOPHER S. TARPLEY (b. 1971) attended Pilchuck Glass School, Stanwood, Washington, and Santa Fe Metalshop, Santa Fe, New Mexico. Experience as goldsmith and lapidary inform signature work in glass, primarily pottery forms. Work draws on multicultural heritage, art of Southwest cultures. Resides in Santa Fe, New Mexico, and Seattle, Washington.

WALTER UFER (1876–1936) claimed he was born in Louisville, Kentucky, but was native of Huckeswagen, Germany. Immigrated with family to Louisville, 1880. Apprenticed with Louisville lithographic firm, went to Germany to study at Dresden Royal Academy. Returned to Chicago to work as illustrator for Armour and Company. In 1911, studied in Munich. Sent to New Mexico in 1914 by Chicago art collectors; returned, 1915, 1916. Moved to Taos, elected to Taos Society of Artists, 1917; served as secretary-treasurer, 1920–22; president, 1922–23. With other Taos and Santa Fe artists formed New Mexico Painters, 1923. Died in Santa Fe.

THEODORE HERBERT "TED" VAN BRUNT (1922–1987) was born in Elmira, New York, attended local schools, graduated from Mechanics Institute of Technology (now Rochester Institute of Technology), 1932. Started art department, Thatcher Glass Corporation, placing designs on glass milk bottles. Ran family car dealership until 1978, taught art classes, received awards from local organizations. Died after extended illness.

BARBARA VAN CLEVE (b. 1935) was born near Big Timber, Montana, and raised on a ranch. When eleven years old, received "Brownie" camera and home developing kit, beginning lifelong interest in photography. Earned advanced degrees in English literature, studied photography at Columbia College, Chicago, 1973–75. Career as college professor, elementary and high school teacher. In 1980, became full-time photographer. Has home and studio in Santa Fe, spends summers on Montana ranch. Inducted into National Cowgirl Hall of Fame, 1995.

THEODORE VAN SOELEN (1890–1964) was born in St. Paul, Minnesota, studied at local Institute of Arts and Sciences, then at Pennsylvania Academy of Fine Arts. In 1916, moved to Albuquerque, New Mexico, for health. Worked as painter and illustrator. Moved to San Ysidro Indian trading post, 1920; moved to Santa Fe, 1922. Observed cowboy life on Texas ranch. Created well-researched historical murals. Elected to National Academy of Design, 1940.

The son of a Portuguese sailor, **CARLOS VIERRA** (1876–1937) was born and raised in Moss Landing, California, near Monterey. Studied at San Francisco Institute, sailed to New York for further study, traveling around Cape Horn. Moved to Santa Fe, 1904, for health, opened photography studio on Plaza. First artist to settle in Santa Fe; founded art colony. Helped restore Museum of New Mexico Palace of the Governors; helped design Museum of Fine Arts building. Painted murals in its St. Francis Auditorium, 1917. Helped create "Santa Fe Style" architecture and design.

HAROLD VON SCHMIDT (1893–1982) was raised in California and moved to New York

in 1924 where he was influenced by Howard Pyle. Contributed to *The Saturday Evening Post* for twenty years.

HAROLD JOE WALDRUM (b. 1934) lives in Taos, New Mexico. He paints fragments of Native American and Hispanic architecture.

Cherokee artist **KAY WALKINGSTICK** (b. 1935) was born in Syracuse, New York. Earned M.F.A., Pratt Institute, 1975; B.F.A, Beaver College, Glenside, Pennsylvania, 1959. Awards include National Honor Award for Outstanding Achievement in the Visual Arts from Women's Caucus for Art, 1996. Best-known for diptychs, her abstractionist work references visual memory, the landscape, women's bodies, contemporary Indian identity. Work represented in numerous prestigious collections, including Metropolitan Museum of Art. Lives in Ithaca and is professor of art, Cornell University.

ANDY WARHOL (1928–1987) was born in Forest City, Pennsylvania, near Pittsburgh, to Czech immigrants. Was best known American Pop artist of his time. Attended Carnegie Institute of Technology in Pittsburgh (now Carnegie-Mellon University). After moving to New York City in the 1940s, worked as magazine illustrator, designed department store windows. Quit commercial art in 1960, destroyed many illustrations. Switched from painting to silk-screen printing; called studio "The Factory." In ten-print series, *Cowboys and Indians* (1986), sought to convey power and irony inherent in enduring symbols of American West.

Born in Wichita Falls, Texas, printmaker and painter **DAVID WHARTON** (b.1951) Received a B.F.A. from the University of Oklahoma, Norman, in 1974, and M.F.A. from Cranbrook Academy of Art, Bloomfield Hills, Missouri, in 1977. Has taught, served as artist-in-residence and lecturer,

mostly in the Pacific Northwest and Alberta, Canada.

SHYATESA WHITE DOVE (b. 1956), Acoma, was born in Albuquerque, New Mexico. She attended the University of New Mexico, 1976–80, and the Institute of American Indian Arts, Santa Fe, 1981–82. Learned traditional Acoma pottery-making techniques from her grandmother, Connie O. Cerno, in 1984. Creates clay sculpture, works in traditional polychrome and black-on-white pottery. Art in collections of School of American Research, Santa Fe, and National Museum of Women in the Arts, Washington, D.C. She lives in Albuquerque.

Navajo painter **EMMI WHITEHORSE** (b. 1956) was born in Crownpoint, New Mexico, on Navajo Reservation. Earned M.A., University of New Mexico, 1982. Known for large abstract panels with multi-layered meaning and media, often including chalk, oil-stick and pigment on paper or canvas. Ethereal mixed-media work explores memory, personal symbology, land, and her Navajo culture. Lives and works in New Mexico.

THOMAS WORTHINGTON WHITTREDGE (1820–1910) was born near Springfield, Ohio, grew up on family farm. Self-taught, was landscape painter in Cincinnati, Ohio, 1843–49. Studied in Dusseldorf in 1849, lived in Rome, 1854–1859. Returned to New York City; elected to National Academy of Design, 1860. Drawn to quiet expression of nature and Native peoples on "Arcadian" Great Plains, preferring them to more dramatic Rocky Mountains. In 1866, accompanied General John Pope on inspection tour of Colorado and New Mexico.

OLAF WIEGHORST (1899–1988) immigrated from Denmark to New York City in 1918. Enlisted in 5th Cavalry, Fort Bliss, Texas; discharged in 1922, became cowboy. Returned to

New York, joined City Mounted Police. After retirement in 1944, began exhibiting paintings of Southwest. Many paintings at National Cowboy and Western Heritage Museum, Oklahoma City. Died in La Mesa, California.

CARL FERDINAND WIMAR (1828–1862) immigrated to St. Louis from Germany in 1843. In early 1850s, went to Germany to study at Dusseldorf Academy. After return to Saint Louis, traveled up Missouri River, mid-1850s; sketched actively. Became best known for *Attack on an Emigrant Train* (1856). Painting became model for similar paintings and Hollywood westerns.

WAYNE E. WOLFE (b. 1945) was born and raised in Kansas City; graduated University of Kansas. In 1973, began to paint part-time; in 1975, gave up advertising career to paint full-time. Self-taught, moved to Santa Fe, 1976, painted with Robert Lougheed, studied with illustrator Tom Lovell. Moved to Monument, Colorado; travels throughout American West, Canada, Europe.

Born in Needham, Massachusetts, **NEWELL CONVERS WYETH** (1882–1945) grew up near Walden Pond, Massachusetts, was encouraged by parents to become artist. Entered Howard Pyle's Brandywine School of American Illustration, 1902. In 1903, *The Saturday Evening Post* published on cover the first illustration he sold. As illustrator for *Scribner's* magazine, traveled west in 1904; returned in 1906. After these trips, created hundreds of illustrations of western life, illustrated children's books. Settled at Chadds Ford, Pennsylvania, became easel painter. In 1930s, painted large murals based on American history. Elected to National Academy of Design, 1941. Killed in car-train accident near Chadd's Ford.

EUSTACE PAUL ZIEGLER (1881–after 1941) was born in Detroit, Michigan, studied at Detroit School of Fine Arts. Settled in Seattle, Washington, worked as painter, muralist, printmaker, teacher. Member, Puget Sound Group of Painters. Painted murals in Alaska and Washington hotels, schools, and libraries.

Other Named Artists in the Collection:

RALPH "TUFFY" BERG (1940–1991), wildlife sculptor.

RICHARD S. BUSWELL, M.D. (b. 1945), photographer, born in Helena, Montana.

TOM CAPOLONGO (n.d.), painter.

MARC DENNIS (b. 1959), painter.

LOUIS FERRETTI (b. 1926), lithographer.

KATIE FISHER, Chemehuevi, basket maker.

LENA GENGE, Navajo, weaver.

B. W. KILBURN (n.d.), photographer.

KURT MARKUS (b. 1947), photographer.

GEORGES FREDERIC ROTIG (1873–1934), painter, born in Netherlands.

SUSANA, San Ildefonso, potter.

BILL WRIGHT (n.d.), photographer.

JUANITA WO-PEAR, Santa Clara, potter.

Rockwell Museum
of Western Art, A History

Like many tales of western adventure, the story of the Rockwell Museum of Western Art began in the Colorado Rockies. Soon after the turn of the twentieth century, Robert F. Rockwell left his native Corning, New York, to become a cattle rancher in western Colorado. His son, Robert (Bob) Rockwell, Jr., grew up on the Colorado ranch but returned to Corning in 1933 to help his grandfather run the family store. In 1940, three years after his marriage to Hertha Godley, Bob took over the Rockwell Department Store.

In 1948, Bob's father established the private Rockwell Foundation in Colorado for educational and charitable purposes. In the 1960s, Bob began to collect western art on behalf of the Foundation. As he learned more about the art he loved, the collection grew rapidly to include works by many of the best-known artists of the nineteenth-and early twentieth-century West. Hertha also became involved in selecting art and artifacts for the collection. Later, their children, Bobby (Robert III) and Sandra, joined in. Before long, works from the Rockwell's American Western Art Collection were exhibited in the family store.

Corning citizens feared they might lose the collection when the Denver Art Museum sought to acquire it in the 1970s. They resolved to

Fig. 4. Corning, New York, City Hall and Fire Department. From the Frank Hewitt Glass Plate Negative Collection (or Hewitt Collection), taken July 1905 during Firemen's Carnival Week, Corning-Painted Post Historical Society, 72.700.29

keep the collection in town, and the Rockwell family agreed to give the community a significant part of the collection if it would establish a museum to house it. In 1976, the Rockwell Museum was founded. The first exhibits were held in the Baron Steuben Hotel building in downtown Corning, attracting thousands of visitors each year.

In 1980, the City of Corning gave the Old City Hall to the Museum. The handsome Romanesque Revival building, erected in 1893, had once housed city offices, the fire station, police station, jail cells, and large community hall. However, after being damaged in a 1972 flood, it had remained empty. Corning Glass Works (now Corning Incorporated) agreed to restore the historic building (listed on the National Register). Other local businesses raised funds to furnish it. In June 1982, the Rockwell Museum opened in the renovated building. For the next eighteen years, the Museum expanded its collections of western art, Carder glass, guns, and antique toys. It also sponsored traveling exhibitions, developed educational programs, published catalogs, and trained a cadre of docents and other volunteers.

In March 2000, the Rockwell Museum's Board of Trustees decided to focus on its fine collection of western and Native American art. Again Corning Incorporated paid for a major renovation. In May 2001, on its twenty-fifth anniversary, the Rockwell Museum of Western Art reopened, offering "The best of the West in the East."

List of Plates

Alphabetical by artist

Plate 86
WILLIAM HERBERT "BUCK" DUNTON
Deer Hunters' Camp (1926)

Plate 47
MICHAEL EASTMAN
Horse #2 (1999)

Plate 49
SETH EASTMAN
The Tanner (1848)

Plate 28
HENRY FARNY
On the Trail in Winter (1894)

Plate 51
HENRY FARNY
The Wailer (1895)

Plate 90
ROSALIE FAVELL
Navigating by Our Grandmothers, from
Plain(s) Warrior Artist (2000)

Plate 85
NICOLAI FECHIN
Sorrento Valley (1925)

Plate 60
EDWARD JAMES FRAUGHTON
The Spirit of Wyoming (1978)

Plate 74
E. MARTIN HENNINGS
The Teacher (c. 1925)

Plate 22
THOMAS HILL
Yosemite (date unknown)

Plate 52
ALLAN HOUSER/HAOZOUS
Apache Gans Dancer (1980)

Plate 18
WILSON HURLEY
La Cueva Cañon, Sandias (1982)

Plate 66
FRANK TENNEY JOHNSON
The Morning Shower (1927)

Plate 81
GENE KLOSS
Song of Creation (1949)

Plate 54
WILLIAM H. D. KOERNER
Tomahawk and Long Rifle (1928)

Plate 20
SYDNEY LAURENCE
Mount McKinley (1922)

Plate 31
WILLIAM ROBINSON LEIGH
The Buffalo Hunt (1947)

Plate 11
WILLIAM ROBINSON LEIGH
The Warning Shadow (1908)

Plate 48
CARM LITTLE TURTLE
Iron Horse (1990/2000)

Plate 1
TRUMAN LOWE
Feather Basket (1989)

Plate 25
TRUMAN LOWE
Feather Basket (1999)

Plate 93
JUDITH LOWRY
Family: Love's Unbreakable Heaven (1995)

Plate 6
MARIO MARTINEZ
Yo Chiva`ato (Enchanted Goat) (1994-1995)

Plate 26
CHRISTINE McHORSE
Rain Bird (1999)

Plate 43
ALFRED JACOB MILLER
Crow Chief on the Lookout (c. 1840)

Plate 5
ALFRED JACOB MILLER
Crow Indian on Horseback (1844)

Plate 7
THOMAS MORAN
Clouds in the Canyon (1915)

Plate 24
THOMAS MORAN
Green River (1877)

Plate 91
JANICE ORTIZ
Zozobra (1999)

Plate 92
LILLIAN PITT
Klicktat Basket with Masks (2000)

Plate 29
OGDEN MINTON PLEISSNER
Lost Lake, Wyoming (c. 1940)

Plate 16
ALEXANDER PROCTOR
The Bull Moose (1903)

Plate 67
FREDERIC REMINGTON
The Arizona Cowboy (1901)

Plate 68
FREDERIC REMINGTON
The Winter Campaign (1909)

Plate 69
FREDERIC REMINGTON
Cutting Out a Steer (1888)

Plate 61
FREDERIC REMINGTON
The Bronco Buster (1895)

For Further Reading

Batkin, Jonathan, ed. *Clay People: Pueblo Indian Figurative Traditions.* Santa Fe: Wheelwright Museum of the American Indian, 1999.

Bickerstaff, Laura M. *Pioneer Artists of Taos.* Denver: Old West Publishing Co., 1955, 1983.

Boehme, Sarah, et. al. *Powerful Images: Portrayals of Native America.* Seattle: University of Washington Press and Museums West, 1998.

Contemporary Masters, The Eiteljorg Fellowship for Native American Fine Art, vol. 1. Indianapolis: Eiteljorg Museum of American Indians and Western Art, 1999.

Craven, Wayne. *Sculpture in America.* New York: Thomas Y. Crowell Company, 1968.

D'Emilio, Sandra, and Suzan Campbell. *Visions & Visionaries: The Art and Artists of the Santa Fe Railway.* Salt Lake City: Peregrine Smith Books, 1991.

Eldredge, Charles C., Julie Schimmel, and William H. Truettner. *Art in New Mexico, 1900–1945: Paths to Santa Fe and Taos.* New York: Abbeville Press, in association with the National Museum of American Art, 1986.

Geist, Valerius. *Buffalo Nation: History and Legend of the North American Bison.* Stillwater, MN: Voyageur Press, 1996.

Goetzmann, William H., and William N. Goetzmann. *The West of the Imagination.* New York: W. W. Norton & Company, 1986.

Hassrick, Peter. *Treasures of the Old West: Paintings and Sculpture from the Thomas Gilcrease Institute of American History and Art.* New York: Abradale Press, Harry N. Abrams, Inc. Publishers, 1984, 1994.

Hassrick, Peter. *The American West: Out of Myth, Into Reality*. Washington, D.C.: Trust for Museum Exhibitions in Association with the Mississippi Museum of Art, 2000.

Hedlund, Ann Lane. *Reflections of the Weaver's World: The Gloria S. Ross Collection of Contemporary Navajo Weaving*. Denver: Denver Art Museum, 1992.

Hobson, Geary, ed. *The Remembered Earth: An Anthology of Contemporary Native American Literature*. Albuquerque: University of New Mexico Press, 1979.

Indian Humor. San Francisco: American Indian Contemporary Arts, 1995.

McMaster, Gerald, ed. *Reservation X: The Power of Place in Aboriginal Contemporary Art*. Seattle: University of Washington Press, 1998.

Nabakov, Peter, ed. Foreword by Vine Deloria, Jr. *Native American Testimony*. New York: Viking, 1978, 1991.

Porter, Dean A., Teresa Hayes Ebie, and Suzan Campbell. *Taos Artists and Their Patrons, 1898-1950*. South Bend, IN: The Snite Museum of Art, University of Notre Dame, 1999.

Rosenak, Chuck and Jan. *The People Speak: Navajo Folk Art*. Flagstaff: Northland Publishing, 1994.

Rushing, W. Jackson, III, ed. *Native American Art in the Twentieth Century: Makers, Meanings, Histories*. London and New York: Routledge, 1999.

Smith, Henry Nash. Virgin Land: *The American West as Symbol and Myth*. Cambridge: Harvard University Press, 1950.

Strong Hearts: Native American Visions and Voices. Aperture, 139 (Summer 1995).

Taft, Robert. *Artists and Illustrators of the Old West, 1850–1900*. 1953; Princeton, N.J.: Princeton University Press, 1982.

Truettner, William H. *The West as America: Reinterpreting Images of the Frontier, 1820–1920*. Washington, D.C.: Smithsonian Institution Press for the National Museum of American Art, 1991.

Troccoli, Joan Carpenter, with Marlene Chambers and Jane Comstock. *Painters and the American West*. New Haven: Yale University Press, in association with the Denver Art Museum, 2000.